A
MEDITATIVE
COMMENTARY
ON THE
NEW TESTAMENT

# LUKE: JESUS IS SAVIOR

A
MEDITATIVE
COMMENTARY
ON THE
NEW TESTAMENT

# LUKE: JESUS IS SAVIOR

by Earl Lavender

LEAFWOOD
PUBLISHERS

LUKE: JESUS IS SAVIOR
Published by Leafwood Publishers

Copyright 2006 by Earl Lavender

ISBN 0-89112-500-0
Printed in the United States of America

Cover design by Greg Jackson, Thinkpen Design, llc

For information:
Leafwood Publishers
1648 Campus Court
Abilene, Texas 79601
1-877-816-4455 (toll free)

Visit our website: www.leafwoodpublishers.com

05 06 07 08 09 10 / 7 6 5 4 3 2 1

*To our children and their spouses:*
*Rachel and Colin, Beth and J.P., and David and Lynn.*
*You have brought us inexpressible joy in your walk with the Lord.*

# C O N T E N T S

**INTRODUCTION:**

**MEDITATIONS:**

# ACKNOWLEDGEMENTS

I am deeply thankful to Gary Holloway for partnering with me in this effort. His work in this series is wonderful. I have already used his commentaries in several classes with great response. I am also thankful to Leonard Allen and Leafwood Publishers. His excitement and support for this effort is a constant encouragement.

A special word of thanks to the Donelson and to Woodmont Hills congregations, who asked me to develop these studies for their use. These brothers and sisters stand as a great example of faith communities committed to the daily study of God's word.

I would also like to offer a special word of thanks to the "early birds" who have for many years so diligently studied the word of God with me every Sunday morning at 7 a.m. As always, none of this work could be done without the wonderful and loving support of Rebecca, my wife. She has taught me more about the truth of Scripture than anyone else has. I will be forever in her debt for her actively living in God's love. She is my constant inspiration.

# INTRODUCTION:

# HEARING GOD IN SCRIPTURE

There are many commentaries, guides, and workbooks on the various books of the Bible. How is this series different? It is not intended to answer all your scholarly questions about the Bible, or even make you an expert in the details of Scripture. Instead, this series is designed to help you hear the voice of God for your everyday life. It is a guide to meditation on the Bible, meditation that will allow the Bible to transform you.

We read in many ways. We might scan the newspaper for information, read a map for location, read a novel for pleasure, or read a textbook to pass a test. These are all good ways to read, depending on our circumstances.

A young soldier far away from home who receives a letter from his wife reads in yet another way. He might scan the letter quickly at first for news and information. But his longing for his beloved causes him to read the letter again and again, hearing her sweet voice in every line. He slowly treasures each word of this precious letter.

## BIBLE STUDY

So also, there are many good ways to read the Bible, depending on our circumstances. Bible study is absolutely necessary for our life with God. We rightly study the Bible for information. We ask, "Who wrote this?" "When was it written?" "Who were the original readers?"

"How do these words apply to me?" More importantly, we want information about God. Who is he? What does he think of me? What does he want from me?

There is no substitute for this kind of close, dedicated Bible study. We must know what the Bible says to know our standing with God. We therefore read the Bible to discover true doctrine or teaching. But some in their emphasis on the authority and inspiration of the Bible have forgotten that Bible study is not an end in itself. We want to know God through Scripture. We want to have a relationship with the Teacher, not just the teachings.

Jesus tells some of God's people in his day, "You diligently study the Scriptures because you think that by them you possess eternal life. These are the Scriptures that testify about me, yet you refuse to come to me to have life" (John 5:39-40). He's not telling them to study their Bibles less, but he is reminding them of the deeper purpose of Bible study—to draw us to God through Jesus. Bible study is a means, not an end.

Yet the way many of us have learned to study the Bible may actually get in the way of hearing God. "Bible study" may sound a lot like schoolwork, and many of us were happy to get out of school. "Bible study" may call to mind pictures of intellectuals surrounded by books in Greek and Hebrew, pondering meanings too deep for ordinary people. The method of Bible study that has been popular for some time focuses on the strangeness of the Bible. It was written long ago, far away, and in languages we cannot read. There is a huge gap between us and the original readers of the Bible, a gap that can only be bridged by scholars, not by average folk.

There is some truth and some value in that "scholarly"method. It is true that the Bible was not written originally to us. Knowing ancient languages and customs can at times help us understand the Bible better. However, one unintended result of this approach is to make the Bible distant from the people of God. We may come to think that we can only hear God indirectly through Scripture, that his word must be filtered through scholars. We may even think that deep Bible study is a matter of mastering obscure information about the Bible.

## MEDITATION

But we read the Bible for more than information. By studying it, we experience transformation, the mysterious process of God at work in us. Through his loving words, God is calling us to life with him. He is forming us into the image of his Son.

Reading the Bible is not like reading other books. We are not simply trying to learn information or master material. Instead, we want to stand under the authority of Scripture and let God master us. While we read the Bible, it reads us, opening the depths of our being to the overpowering love of God. "For the word of God is living and active. Sharper than any double-edged sword, it penetrates even to dividing soul and spirit, joints and marrow; it judges the thoughts and attitudes of the heart. Nothing in all creation is hidden from God's sight. Everything is uncovered and laid bare before the eyes of him to whom we must give account" (Hebrews 4:12-13).

Opening our hearts to the word of God is meditation. Although this way of reading the Bible may be new to some, it has a long heritage among God's people. The Psalmist joyously meditates on the words of God (Psalm 1:2; 39:3; 119:15, 23, 27, 48, 78, 97, 99, 148). Meditation is taking the words of Scripture to heart and letting them ask questions of us. It is slowly chewing over a text, listening closely, reading God's message of love to us over and over. This is not a simple, easy, or naïve reading of Scripture, but a process that takes time, dedication, and practice on our part.

There are many ways to meditate on the Bible. One is praying the Scriptures. Prayer and Bible study really cannot be separated. One way of praying the Bible is to make the words of a text your prayer. Obviously, the prayer texts of Scripture, especially the Psalms, lend themselves to this. "The Lord is my shepherd" has been the prayer of many hearts.

However, it is proper and helpful to turn the words of the Bible into prayers. Commands from God can become prayers. "You shall have no other gods before me" (Exodus 20:3) can be prayed, "Lord, keep me from anything that takes your place in my heart." Stories can be prayed. Jesus heals a man born blind (John 9), and so we pray, "Lord Jesus open my eyes to who you truly are." Even the promises of the Bible become prayers. "Never will I leave you; never will I forsake you" (Deuteronomy 31:6; Hebrews 13:5) becomes "God help me know that you promise that you are always with me and so live my life without fear."

Obviously, there are many helpful ways of hearing the voice of God in Scripture. Again, the purpose of Bible reading and study is not to know more about the Bible, much less to pride ourselves as experts on Scripture. Instead, we read to hear the voice of our Beloved. We listen for a word of God for us.

## HOLY READING

This commentary reflects one ancient way of meditation and praying the Scriptures known as *lectio divina* or holy reading. This method assumes that God wants to speak to us directly in the Bible, that the passage we are reading is God's word to us right now. The writers of the New Testament read the Old Testament with this same conviction. They saw the words of the Bible speaking directly to their own situation. They read with humility and with prayer.

The first step along this way of holy reading is listening to the Bible. Choose a biblical text that is not too long. This commentary breaks Luke into smaller sections. The purpose is to hear God's voice in your current situation, not to cover material or prepare lessons. Get into a comfortable position and maintain silence before God for several minutes. This prepares the heart to listen. Read slowly. Savor each word. Perhaps read aloud. Listen for a particular phrase that speaks to you. Ask God, "What are you trying to tell me today?"

The next step is to meditate on that particular phrase. That meditation may include slowly repeating the phrase that seems to be for you today. As you think deeply on it, you might even memorize it. Committing biblical passages to memory allows us to hold them in our hearts all day long. If you keep a journal, you might write the passage there. Let those words sink deeply into your heart.

Then pray those words back to God in your heart. Those words may call up visual images, smells, sounds, and feelings. Pay attention to what God is giving you in those words. Then respond in faith to what those words say to your heart. What do they call you to be and to do? Our humble response might take the form of praise, thanksgiving, joy, confession, or even cries of pain.

The final step in this "holy reading" is contemplation of God. The words from God that we receive deeply in our hearts lead us to him. Through these words, we experience union with the all-powerful God of love. Again, one should not separate Bible reading from prayer. The words of God in Scripture transport us into the very presence of God where we joyfully rest in his love.

What keeps reading the Bible this way from becoming merely our own desires read back into Scripture? How do we know it is God's voice we hear and not our own?

Two things. One is prayer. We are asking God to open our hearts, minds, and lives to him. We ask to hear his voice, not ours and not the voice of the world around us.

The second thing that keeps this from being an exercise in self-deception is to study the Bible in community. By praying over

Scripture in a group, we hear God's word together. God speaks through the other members of our group. The wisdom he gives them keeps us from private, selfish, and unusual interpretations. They help us keep our own voices in check, as we desire to listen to God alone.

## HOW TO USE THIS COMMENTARY

This commentary provides assistance in holy reading of the Bible. It gives structure to daily personal devotions, family meditation, small group Bible studies, and church classes.

### DAILY DEVOTIONAL

Listening, meditation, prayer, contemplation. How does this commentary fit into this way of Bible study? Consider it as a conversation partner. We have taken a section of Scripture and then broken it down into four short daily readings. After listening, meditating, praying, and contemplating the passage for the day, use the questions suggested in the commentary to provoke deeper reflection. This provides a structure for a daily fifteen minute devotional four days a week. On the fifth day, read the entire passage, meditate, and then use the questions to reflect on the meaning of the whole. On day six, take our meditations on the passage as conversation with another who has prayed over the text.

If you want to begin daily Bible reading, but need guidance, this provides a Monday-Saturday experience that prepares the heart for worship and praise on Sunday. This structure also results in a communal reading of Scripture, instead of a private reading. Even if you use this commentary alone, you are not reading privately. God is at work in you and in the conversation you have with another (the author of the commentary) who has sought to hear God through this particular passage of the Bible.

## FAMILY BIBLE STUDY

This commentary can also provide an arrangement for family Bible study. Many Christian parents want to lead their children in daily study, but don't know where to begin or how to structure their time. Using the six-day plan outlined above means the entire family can read, meditate, pray, and reflect on the shorter passages, using the questions provided. On day five, they can review the entire passage, and then on day six, read the meditations in the commentary to prompt reflection and discussion. God will bless our families beyond our imaginations through the prayerful study of his word.

## WEEKLY GROUP STUDY

This commentary can also structure small group Bible study. Each member of the group should have meditated over the daily readings and questions for the five days preceding the group meeting, using the method outlined above. The day before the group meeting, each member should read and reflect on the meditations in the commentary on that passage. You then can meet once a week to hear God's word together. In that group meeting, the method of holy reading would look something like this:

*Listening*
    1) Five minutes of silence.
    2) Slow reading of the biblical passage for that week.
    3) A minute of silent meditation on the passage.

4) Briefly share with the group the word or phrase that struck you.

*Personal Message*
   5) A second reading of the same passage.
   6) A minute of silence.
   7) Where does this touch your life today?
   8) Responses: I hear, I see, etc.

*Life Response*
   9) Brief silence.
   10) What does God want you to do today in light of this word?

*Group Prayer*
   11) Have each member of the group pray aloud for the person on
       his or her left, asking God to bless the word he has given them.

The procedure suggested here can be used in churches or in neighborhood Bible studies. Church members would use the daily readings Monday-Friday in their daily devotionals. This commentary intentionally provides no readings on the sixth day, so that we can spend Saturdays as a time of rest, not rest from Bible study, but a time to let God's word quietly work its way deep into our hearts. Sunday during Bible school or in home meetings, the group would meet to experience the weekly readings together, using the group method described above. It might be that the sermon for each Sunday could be on the passage for that week.

There are churches that have used this structure to great advantage. In the hallways of those church buildings, the talk is not of the local football team or the weather, but of the shared experience of the Word of God for that week.

And that is the purpose of our personal and communal study, to hear the voice of God, our loving Father who wants us to love him in return. He deeply desires a personal relationship with us. Father, Son, and Spirit make a home inside us (see John 14:16-17, 23). Our loving God speaks to his children! But we must listen for his voice. That listening is not a matter of gritting our teeth and trying harder to hear. Instead, it is part of our entire life with God. That is what Bible study is all about.

Through daily personal prayer and meditation on God's word and through a communal reading of Scripture, our most important conversation partner, the Holy Spirit, will do his mysterious and marvelous work. Among other things, the Spirit pours God's love into our hearts (Romans 5:5), bears witness to our spirits that we are God's children (Romans 8:16), intercedes for us with God (Romans 8:26), and enlightens us as to God's will (Ephesians 1:17).

So this is an invitation to personal daily Bible study, to praying the Scriptures, to sharing with fellow believers, to hear the voice of God. God will bless us, our families, our churches, and his world if we take the time to be still, listen, and do his word.

# THE SPIRITUALITY OF LUKE

Luke is the first of a two-part work. Along with Acts, it tells the exciting story of God breaking into human history by establishing his kingdom. This is not a new story, but the continuation of God's purposes from creation. Luke/Acts is an invitation for us to join the story. Luke is not concerned with merely presenting information about the life of Jesus; he wants us to see Jesus as Savior of the world. And he wants us to know that the salvation Jesus brings is not a formal religion, but life in relationship with God. In Jesus, God calls us to live life to the fullest. He calls us to return to the life for which he created us.

Jesus is the perfect manifestation of that life, a life that finds its meaning in fully submitting to the will of the God who created us. It is a life focused on fulfilling the mission of God to the world.

## THE ROLE OF THE HOLY SPIRIT IN THE MINISTRY OF JESUS

The Holy Spirit plays a major role in Luke and Acts. From the beginning of the story of Jesus, the Holy Spirit fills and directs the lives of those in God's plans. He fills Zechariah and Elizabeth before the birth of John the Baptist. He fills Mary and causes the miraculous birth of Jesus. The Spirit was on Simeon when he praised the Christ child at the temple. John the Baptist prophesies that the one who follows him will baptize with the Holy Spirit. The Holy Spirit descends like a dove on Jesus at his baptism. The Holy Spirit continues to direct the actions and words of Jesus throughout his ministry. In Acts, the Spirit moves into the major role, guiding the disciples to act and speak like Jesus.

## REACHING OUT TO THE SOCIALLY MARGINALIZED

The focus, which most sets Luke apart from the other gospels, is that of his concern for those marginalized by their culture. In the birth narrative alone, Luke points out that an older couple without children (which would be cause for the wife to be ostracized) are the first to be blessed by the story. Mary, a young virgin from a small town, is chosen to give birth to the Messiah. Shepherds are called to attest to the magnificent event (they were considered crude, unlearned, liars, and unclean). An old man and an elderly widow bless the infant Jesus at the temple. When Jesus announces his ministry in Luke 4, he recites Isaiah's words "The Spirit of the

Lord is on me, because he has anointed me to preach good news to the poor." Lepers are touched, sinful women forgiven, the blind are given sight, the widow's son is "given back to her." A woman with a bleeding problem (hence "unclean") is healed without rebuke, children (considered worthless in that day) are blessed and exalted by Jesus as examples of kingdom life. If we are to know Jesus as Luke saw him, we must learn to love those he loved, to touch those he touched, to help those he helped.

## LIFE RESTORED! JESUS IS SAVIOR

The language of Luke points to Jesus' concern to return those who are hurting to full life. Even before his birth, Elizabeth acknowledges that in giving birth to John, the Lord has "shown his favor and taken away my disgrace among the people" (Luke 1:25). Throughout the story of Jesus, he is restoring life to the broken. The widow of Nain's son is "given back to her." Life restored! The paralytic is not only healed, but also given the strength and coordination to pick up his mat and go home! Life restored! The man possessed by a legion of demons is found sitting at Jesus' feet, nicely dressed and in his right mind. Life restored! Jesus heals and confers peace on those who came to him in faith.

From Luke 2:11 on, it is clear that Jesus is savior. After dining at Zacchaeus' house, Jesus states the purpose of his coming as seeking and saving the lost (19:10). The salvation he offers is much more than just an opportunity for hope in the after life – it is the full restoration to life in God's kingdom – now. Luke wants his readers to know that whatever they have suffered, wherever they are spiritually, Jesus can and will heal. All we need to do is come to him in faith.

## THE SPIRITUALITY OF JESUS

One cannot read Luke without being deeply impressed by the spiritual disciplines of Jesus himself. Luke clearly emphasizes the prayer life of Jesus more than the other gospel accounts. Jesus prays, many times through the night, before making major decisions. Jesus constantly sought solitude. It was time alone with God that gave Jesus the strength to engage fully in his ministry to humanity.

Luke challenges us to embrace the spiritual disciplines of Jesus. It is clear that Jesus is not praying to provide an example to us. He is praying because he knows who he is and what he needs. We would do well to take special notice of when and what Jesus prayed. His prayer from the cross (recorded only in Luke) may shock us. How could he pray for the forgiveness of those who were intentionally causing him so much pain and anguish? If you begin reading the story taking note of all the times Jesus prayed, his prayer from the cross is no longer so difficult to comprehend. Only a life cultivated in continual prayer to God and the constant seeking of his presence could produce such profound demonstrations of grace and mercy in the midst of such suffering.

Consider one last thought concerning the spirituality of Luke's account. The table is a major feature in Luke and Acts. Eating was a central event in the world of Jesus. It was the place of claiming status. It was the place of demonstrating high standing and acceptance. It was also a place to convey disapproval towards "sinners." Some have suggested Jesus was killed as much for his table manners as anything. There is truth in this. Jesus would not tolerate the "closed table" system of his day. All were welcomed. Even sinners. Especially sinners. Jesus demonstrates to us that when one spends much time in prayer and solitude – alone with God – the result is an open heart and a profoundly inviting hospitality.

# THE STORY BEGINS

## (Luke 1)

### Day One Reading and Questions:

¹ Many have undertaken to draw up an account of the things that have been fulfilled among us, ² just as they were handed down to us by those who from the first were eyewitnesses and servants of the word. ³ Therefore, since I myself have carefully investigated everything from the beginning, it seemed good also to me to write an orderly account for you, most excellent Theophilus, ⁴ so that you may know the certainty of the things you have been taught.

⁵ In the time of Herod king of Judea there was a priest named Zechariah, who belonged to the priestly division of Abijah; his wife Elizabeth was also a descendant of Aaron. ⁶ Both of them were upright in the sight of God, observing all the Lord's commandments and regulations blamelessly. ⁷ But they had no children, because Elizabeth was barren; and they were both well along in years.

⁸ Once when Zechariah's division was on duty and he was serving as priest before God, ⁹ he was chosen by lot, according to the custom of the priesthood, to go into the temple of the Lord and burn incense. ¹⁰ And when the time for the burning of incense came, all the assembled worshipers were praying outside.

¹¹ Then an angel of the Lord appeared to him, standing at the right side of the altar of incense. ¹² When Zechariah saw him, he was startled and was gripped with fear. ¹³ But the angel said to him: "Do not be afraid, Zechariah; your prayer has been heard. Your wife

Elizabeth will bear you a son, and you are to give him the name John. [14] He will be a joy and delight to you, and many will rejoice because of his birth, [15] for he will be great in the sight of the Lord. He is never to take wine or other fermented drink, and he will be filled with the Holy Spirit even from birth. [16] Many of the people of Israel will he bring back to the Lord their God. [17] And he will go on before the Lord, in the spirit and power of Elijah, to turn the hearts of the fathers to their children and the disobedient to the wisdom of the righteous—to make ready a people prepared for the Lord."

[18] Zechariah asked the angel, "How can I be sure of this? I am an old man and my wife is well along in years."

[19] The angel answered, "I am Gabriel. I stand in the presence of God, and I have been sent to speak to you and to tell you this good news. [20] And now you will be silent and not able to speak until the day this happens, because you did not believe my words, which will come true at their proper time."

*1. To whom did Luke address this work? What is his purpose in writing it?*

*2. Why do you think God chose Elizabeth and Zechariah to give birth to John?*

*3. Would you have reacted as Zechariah to such a surprising turn of events? What has God done in your life that caught you by surprise?*

## DAY TWO READING AND QUESTIONS:

[21] Meanwhile, the people were waiting for Zechariah and wondering why he stayed so long in the temple. [22] When he came out, he could not speak to them. They realized he had seen a vision in the

temple, for he kept making signs to them but remained unable to speak.

[23] When his time of service was completed, he returned home. [24] After this his wife Elizabeth became pregnant and for five months remained in seclusion. [25] "The Lord has done this for me," she said. "In these days he has shown his favor and taken away my disgrace among the people."

[26] In the sixth month, God sent the angel Gabriel to Nazareth, a town in Galilee, [27] to a virgin pledged to be married to a man named Joseph, a descendant of David. The virgin's name was Mary. [28] The angel went to her and said, "Greetings, you who are highly favored! The Lord is with you."

[29] Mary was greatly troubled at his words and wondered what kind of greeting this might be. [30] But the angel said to her, "Do not be afraid, Mary, you have found favor with God. [31] You will be with child and give birth to a son, and you are to give him the name Jesus. [32] He will be great and will be called the Son of the Most High. The Lord God will give him the throne of his father David, [33] and he will reign over the house of Jacob forever; his kingdom will never end."

[34] "How will this be," Mary asked the angel, "since I am a virgin?"

[35] The angel answered, "The Holy Spirit will come upon you, and the power of the Most High will overshadow you. So the holy one to be born will be called the Son of God. [36] Even Elizabeth your relative is going to have a child in her old age, and she who was said to be barren is in her sixth month. [37] For nothing is impossible with God."

[38] "I am the Lord's servant," Mary answered. "May it be to me as you have said." Then the angel left her.

*1. Why do you think Elizabeth remained in seclusion for five months?*

*2. How did Mary's reaction differ from Zechariah's?*

*3. What does Mary's answer reflect about her relationship with God?*

## DAY THREE READING AND QUESTIONS:

[39] At that time Mary got ready and hurried to a town in the hill country of Judea, [40] where she entered Zechariah's home and greeted Elizabeth. [41] When Elizabeth heard Mary's greeting, the baby leaped in her womb, and Elizabeth was filled with the Holy Spirit. [42] In a loud voice she exclaimed: "Blessed are you among women, and blessed is the child you will bear! [43] But why am I so favored, that the mother of my Lord should come to me? [44] As soon as the sound of your greeting reached my ears, the baby in my womb leaped for joy. [45] Blessed is she who has believed that what the Lord has said to her will be accomplished!"

[46] And Mary said:

"My soul glorifies the Lord
[47] and my spirit rejoices in God my Savior,
[48] for he has been mindful
    of the humble state of his servant.
    from now on all generations will call me blessed,
[49] for the Mighty One has done great things for me—
    holy is his name.
[50] His mercy extends to those who fear him,
    from generation to generation.
[51] He has performed mighty deeds with his arm;
    he has scattered those who are proud in their inmost thoughts.
[52] He has brought down rulers from their thrones
    but has lifted up the humble.
[53] He has filled the hungry with good things
    but has sent the rich away empty.
[54] He has helped his servant Israel,
    remembering to be merciful
[55] to Abraham and his descendants forever,

even as he said to our fathers."
⁵⁶ Mary stayed with Elizabeth for about three months and then returned home.

*1. Why did Elizabeth call Mary "blessed"?*

*2. What does Mary's song reveal to us about her faith?*

*3. Why do you think Mary focuses on "great reversals" in her song? (scattered the proud, lifted the humble, sent the rich away)*

## DAY FOUR READING AND QUESTIONS:

⁵⁷ When it was time for Elizabeth to have her baby, she gave birth to a son. ⁵⁸ Her neighbors and relatives heard that the Lord had shown her great mercy, and they shared her joy.

⁵⁹ On the eighth day they came to circumcise the child, and they were going to name him after his father Zechariah, ⁶⁰ but his mother spoke up and said, "No! He is to be called John."

⁶¹ They said to her, "There is no one among your relatives who has that name."

⁶² Then they made signs to his father, to find out what he would like to name the child. ⁶³ He asked for a writing tablet, and to everyone's astonishment he wrote, "His name is John." ⁶⁴ Immediately his mouth was opened and his tongue was loosed, and he began to speak, praising God. ⁶⁵ The neighbors were all filled with awe, and throughout the hill country of Judea people were talking about all these things. ⁶⁶ Everyone who heard this wondered about it, asking, "What then is this child going to be?" For the Lord's hand was with him.

⁶⁷ His father Zechariah was filled with the Holy Spirit and prophesied:

[68] "Praise be to the Lord, the God of Israel,
    because he has come and has redeemed his people.
[69] He has raised up a horn of salvation for us
    in the house of his servant David
[70] (as he said through his holy prophets of long ago),
[71] salvation from our enemies
    and from the hand of all who hate us—
[72] to show mercy to our fathers
    and to remember his holy covenant,
[73] the oath he swore to our father Abraham:
[74] to rescue us from the hand of our enemies,
    and to enable us to serve him without fear
[75] in holiness and righteousness before him all our days.
[76] And you, my child, will be called a prophet of the Most High;
    for you will go on before the Lord to prepare the way for him,
[77] to give his people the knowledge of salvation
    through the forgiveness of their sins,
[78] because of the tender mercy of our God,
    by which the rising sun will come to us from heaven
[79] to shine on those living in darkness
    and in the shadow of death,
    to guide our feet into the path of peace."
[80] And the child grew and became strong in spirit; and he lived in the desert until he appeared publicly to Israel.

*1. What was the first thing Zechariah did when he recovered his ability to speak?*

*2. What does Zechariah's song have in common with Mary's?*

*3. What did Zechariah understand to be his son's purpose?*

## Day Five Reading and Questions:

Reread the entire passage (1:1-80)

1. *If an angel had appeared announcing your birth, what do you think he would have identified as the purpose of your life?*

2. *What strikes you as most meaningful in this first chapter of Luke's gospel? Most surprising?*

3. *Consider the many blessings you have received from God. Write a song of praise to God for your life. How does it compare to Mary's and Zechariah's songs?*

# MEDITATION

Right from the beginning of Luke's account, we encounter "the great reversal" that dominates his telling of the story. Zechariah and Elizabeth were elderly and marginalized by their culture. Elizabeth carried the heavy burden of not being able to bear a child. They had doubtlessly prayed many times for children. In their day, barrenness indicated disfavor with God. Yet, they were the ones chosen to begin this marvelous story.

Picture yourself as Zechariah, walking into the temple to burn incense. He had the prayer on his heart that he had brought to God many times. When the angel Gabriel appeared (filling Zechariah with fear) he told Zechariah his prayer had been heard and he would be given a son. Ironically, it was not only Zechariah and Elizabeth who were praying for the son they would be given. All of Israel had prayed for this child to be born! He would be the one to prepare the way for the Messiah!

Why did Zechariah doubt? Was he afraid the angel was misleading him? Was this message simply too good to be true? God is a surprising God, is he not? Compare Zechariah's response to that of Mary. While Zechariah and Elizabeth were too old to have a child, Mary was too young. She was not yet married and was a virgin. But Gabriel told her she would have a child. Her question was similar to Zechariah's—"How can this be?" Her response thrills our hearts and explains why she was the one chosen to give birth to the Messiah; "I am the Lord's servant, may it be to me as you have said."

How would we respond to God if we were told of something of this magnitude that would dramatically change the course of our lives? Would we doubt and ask for proof as did Zechariah? Or would we submit willingly to the call of our God? We make this choice daily. Either we choose to submit fully to God's direction, or we live in the world of our own making. These are very different worlds. Our self-directed life is full of limitations, but all things are possible when we live where God is in control.

It is significant that songs of praise surround the birth of Jesus. Mary's and Zechariah's songs remind us of the songs of Moses and Miriam. When God delivers in a mighty way, the natural reaction of the one saved is to praise the deliverer passionately.

"Great Deliverer, help us remember how you have faithfully freed us from those who would destroy us. Fill our hearts with song as we meditate on the joy surrounding the birth of John and Jesus."

# THE MESSIAH IS BORN

## (Luke 2)

### DAY ONE READING AND QUESTIONS:

¹ In those days Caesar Augustus issued a decree that a census should be taken of the entire Roman world. ² (This was the first census that took place while Quirinius was governor of Syria.) ³ And everyone went to his own town to register.

⁴ So Joseph also went up from the town of Nazareth in Galilee to Judea, to Bethlehem the town of David, because he belonged to the house and line of David. ⁵ He went there to register with Mary, who was pledged to be married to him and was expecting a child. ⁶ While they were there, the time came for the baby to be born, ⁷ and she gave birth to her firstborn, a son. She wrapped him in cloths and placed him in a manger, because there was no room for them in the inn.

*1. Why do you think Luke mentions the census as a reference point for Jesus' birth?*

*2. Does Luke give the impression that Jesus was born as soon as they arrived—or were they already there when the time came?*

*3. Do you see the contrast in these verses between those in power and those seemingly without power? What might this tell us?*

## Day Two Reading and Questions:

[8] And there were shepherds living out in the fields nearby, keeping watch over their flocks at night. [9] An angel of the Lord appeared to them, and the glory of the Lord shone around them, and they were terrified. [10] But the angel said to them, "Do not be afraid. I bring you good news of great joy that will be for all the people. [11] Today in the town of David a Savior has been born to you; he is Christ the Lord. [12] This will be a sign to you: You will find a baby wrapped in cloths and lying in a manger."

[13] Suddenly a great company of the heavenly host appeared with the angel, praising God and saying,

[14] "Glory to God in the highest,
    and on earth peace to men on whom his favor rests."

[15] When the angels had left them and gone into heaven, the shepherds said to one another, "Let's go to Bethlehem and see this thing that has happened which the Lord has told us about."

[16] So they hurried off and found Mary and Joseph, and the baby, who was lying in the manger. [17] When they had seen him, they spread the word concerning what had been told them about this child, [18] and all who heard it were amazed at what the shepherds said to them. [19] But Mary treasured up all these things and pondered them in her heart. [20] The shepherds returned, glorifying and praising God for all the things they had heard and seen, which were just as they had been told.

1. *Why did the appearance of the angel cause fear? What was the angel's message?*

2. *To whom did the shepherds attribute the message? What did they do?*

3. *What was the reaction of the shepherds as they returned to their flocks? Why?*

## Day Three Reading and Questions:

[21] On the eighth day, when it was time to circumcise him, he was named Jesus, the name the angel had given him before he had been conceived.

[22] When the time of their purification according to the Law of Moses had been completed, Joseph and Mary took him to Jerusalem to present him to the Lord [23] (as it is written in the Law of the Lord, "Every firstborn male is to be consecrated to the Lord" ), [24] and to offer a sacrifice in keeping with what is said in the Law of the Lord: "a pair of doves or two young pigeons."

[25] Now there was a man in Jerusalem called Simeon, who was righteous and devout. He was waiting for the consolation of Israel, and the Holy Spirit was upon him. [26] It had been revealed to him by the Holy Spirit that he would not die before he had seen the Lord's Christ. [27] Moved by the Spirit, he went into the temple courts. When the parents brought in the child Jesus to do for him what the custom of the Law required, [28] Simeon took him in his arms and praised God, saying:

[29] "Sovereign Lord, as you have promised,
   you now dismiss your servant in peace.
[30] For my eyes have seen your salvation,
[31] which you have prepared in the sight of all people,
[32] a light for revelation to the Gentiles
   and for glory to your people Israel."

[33] The child's father and mother marveled at what was said about him. [34] Then Simeon blessed them and said to Mary, his mother: "This child is destined to cause the falling and rising of many in Israel, and to be a sign that will be spoken against, [35] so that the thoughts of many hearts will be revealed. And a sword will pierce your own soul too."

[36] There was also a prophetess, Anna, the daughter of Phanuel, of the tribe of Asher. She was very old; she had lived with her husband

seven years after her marriage, [37] and then was a widow until she was eighty-four. She never left the temple but worshiped night and day, fasting and praying. [38] Coming up to them at that very moment, she gave thanks to God and spoke about the child to all who were looking forward to the redemption of Jerusalem.

[39] When Joseph and Mary had done everything required by the Law of the Lord, they returned to Galilee to their own town of Nazareth. [40] And the child grew and became strong; he was filled with wisdom, and the grace of God was upon him.

1. *What does the action of Joseph and Mary tell us about their understanding of the Law (see verse 39 as well)? Why is this important?*

2. *Why does Simeon tell us of the purpose of Jesus? To whom shall he bring salvation?*

3. *How does Luke characterize the early years of Jesus?*

## DAY FOUR READING AND QUESTIONS:

[41] Every year his parents went to Jerusalem for the Feast of the Passover. [42] When he was twelve years old, they went up to the Feast, according to the custom. [43] After the Feast was over, while his parents were returning home, the boy Jesus stayed behind in Jerusalem, but they were unaware of it. [44] Thinking he was in their company, they traveled on for a day. Then they began looking for him among their relatives and friends. [45] When they did not find him, they went back to Jerusalem to look for him. [46] After three days they found him in the temple courts, sitting among the teachers, listening to them and asking them questions. [47] Everyone who heard him was amazed at his understanding and his answers. [48] When his parents saw him, they

were astonished. His mother said to him, "Son, why have you treated us like this? Your father and I have been anxiously searching for you."

[49] "Why were you searching for me?" he asked. "Didn't you know I had to be in my Father's house?" [50] But they did not understand what he was saying to them.

[51] Then he went down to Nazareth with them and was obedient to them. But his mother treasured all these things in her heart. [52] And Jesus grew in wisdom and stature, and in favor with God and men.

*1. Why do you think Luke included this episode in the life of Jesus?*

*2. What was Jesus doing among the teachers? What does this tell us about Jesus?*

*3. How does Luke characterize the later years of Jesus' growth into manhood?*

## Day Five Reading and Questions:

Reread the entire passage (2:1-52)

*1. What does the manger tell us about those things we deem so valuable in our world?*

*2. Imagine being one of the shepherds who heard the heavenly host. Can you experience the thrill of participating in such an adventure? What would you have said to the people in Bethlehem that night?*

*3. How can we cultivate hearts similar to those of Simeon and Anna? Do you know anyone who reminds you of Simeon and Anna? Consider the qualities of their lives.*

# MEDITATION

The most significant birth in history occurred in a stable! Luke begins the story of Jesus' birth with information we get from no other gospel. He wants to make sure his readers understand that all the ideas of importance and status are broken from the very beginning of the Savior's life.

Shepherds were social outcasts in Jesus' time. They were dirty, considered unclean, and known to be untruthful. Yet it was to shepherds that the angel, along with a great company of heavenly host, appeared and announced the wondrous event. God chose them to attest to the birth of the Savior, the Messiah Lord. And they were to find the child in a feeding trough! It was exactly as they had been told. They returned to their flocks rejoicing for all the things they had seen and heard. "Seen and heard" are important words to Luke, for there would be many who would not see and not hear. As we study through Luke's account, take notice of those who see and hear and those who don't. It is not who we would think.

That theme continues as they take the child to the temple to be consecrated. Among all the religious leaders around the temple, of all the priests and scholars, only Simeon and Anna knew who had come. How did they know? Simeon was a righteous and devout man, waiting for the consolation of Israel. The Holy Spirit revealed to him that he would see the salvation of the Lord. And so he did! Anna fasted, prayed and worshiped day and night—and so she knew as well.

All the way through this wonderful story, those who seek the Lord in faith are not disappointed. What is heart breaking is how few seek him. Where would we be in this story? What are the spiritual disciplines in our daily lives that demonstrate our great desire to know the will of the Lord? Granted, God appears to whomever he chooses. Luke does not reveal a reason that the angel appeared to the shepherds.

God sometimes just surprises people with his mercy. We do know, however, why Simeon and Anna participated in the story. They constantly sought the will of God, fully engaging in the disciplines of study, prayer, fasting and worship.

Luke gives us a brief snapshot of Jesus' childhood. He grew in wisdom and strength. Then at the age of twelve, we see his deep passion for learning more about his Father's house. He is among the teachers, listening and asking questions. After this brief episode, we see again that Jesus grew in wisdom and stature. The stage is set. No one would have expected this beginning. And few were prepared to hear and see what was to come. Have we seen? Have we heard?

"Lord, open our hearts to hear what you would teach us. Open our eyes to see our world as you see it. May we grow in wisdom, proclaiming the message of a Savior who has come."

# PREPARING THE WAY

## (Luke 3)

### DAY ONE READING AND QUESTIONS:

[1] In the fifteenth year of the reign of Tiberius Caesar—when Pontius Pilate was governor of Judea, Herod tetrarch of Galilee, his brother Philip tetrarch of Iturea and Traconitis, and Lysanias tetrarch of Abilene— [2] during the high priesthood of Annas and Caiaphas, the word of God came to John son of Zechariah in the desert. [3] He went into all the country around the Jordan, preaching a baptism of repentance for the forgiveness of sins.

*1. What "historical marker" does Luke provide in these verses? Why is this significant?*

*2. What was the purpose of John's baptism? What does "repentance" mean to you?*

*3. Can you remember "historical markers" surrounding your obedience to the gospel? If someone would write a history of your life from that point, how would it begin?*

### DAY TWO READING AND QUESTIONS:

[4] As it is written in the book of the words of Isaiah the prophet:
  "A voice of one calling in the desert,

'Prepare the way for the Lord,
    make straight paths for him.
[5] Every valley shall be filled in,
    every mountain and hill made low.
The crooked roads shall become straight,
    the rough ways smooth.
        [6] And all mankind will see God's salvation.' "

[7] John said to the crowds coming out to be baptized by him, "You brood of vipers! Who warned you to flee from the coming wrath? [8] Produce fruit in keeping with repentance. And do not begin to say to yourselves, 'We have Abraham as our father.' For I tell you that out of these stones God can raise up children for Abraham. [9] The ax is already at the root of the trees, and every tree that does not produce good fruit will be cut down and thrown into the fire."

[10] "What should we do then?" the crowd asked.

[11] John answered, "The man with two tunics should share with him who has none, and the one who has food should do the same."

[12] Tax collectors also came to be baptized. "Teacher," they asked, "what should we do?"

[13] "Don't collect any more than you are required to," he told them.

[14] Then some soldiers asked him, "And what should we do?"
He replied, "Don't extort money and don't accuse people falsely—be content with your pay."

1. *According to Isaiah, what was the purpose of John's work?*

2. *How would you describe John's approach to preaching?*

3. *If we were to ask John what we should do, in our vocation, in order to "bear fruits of repentance," what do you think he would say to us?*

## DAY THREE READING AND QUESTIONS:

[15] The people were waiting expectantly and were all wondering in their hearts if John might possibly be the Christ. [16] John answered them all, "I baptize you with water. But one more powerful than I will come, the thongs of whose sandals I am not worthy to untie. He will baptize you with the Holy Spirit and with fire. [17] His winnowing fork is in his hand to clear his threshing floor and to gather the wheat into his barn, but he will burn up the chaff with unquenchable fire." [18] And with many other words John exhorted the people and preached the good news to them.

[19] But when John rebuked Herod the tetrarch because of Herodias, his brother's wife, and all the other evil things he had done, [20] Herod added this to them all: He locked John up in prison.

*1. Why do you think people were considering the possibility of John being the Messiah?*

*2. What was the difference between John's baptism and that of Jesus? What do you think this means?*

*3. What was the good news John proclaimed to the people?*

## DAY FOUR READING AND QUESTIONS:

[21] When all the people were being baptized, Jesus was baptized too. And as he was praying, heaven was opened [22] and the Holy Spirit descended on him in bodily form like a dove. And a voice came from heaven: "You are my Son, whom I love; with you I am well pleased."

[23] Now Jesus himself was about thirty years old when he began his

ministry. He was the son, so it was thought, of Joseph,

the son of Heli, [24] the son of Matthat,

the son of Levi, the son of Melki,

the son of Jannai, the son of Joseph,

[25] the son of Mattathias, the son of Amos,

the son of Nahum, the son of Esli,

the son of Naggai, [26] the son of Maath,

the son of Mattathias, the son of Semein,

the son of Josech, the son of Joda,

[27] the son of Joanan, the son of Rhesa,

the son of Zerubbabel, the son of Shealtiel,

the son of Neri, [28] the son of Melki,

the son of Addi, the son of Cosam,

the son of Elmadam, the son of Er,

[29] the son of Joshua, the son of Eliezer,

the son of Jorim, the son of Matthat,

the son of Levi, [30] the son of Simeon,

the son of Judah, the son of Joseph,

the son of Jonam, the son of Eliakim,

[31] the son of Melea, the son of Menna,

the son of Mattatha, the son of Nathan,

the son of David, [32] the son of Jesse,

the son of Obed, the son of Boaz,

the son of Salmon, the son of Nahshon,

[33] the son of Amminadab, the son of Ram,

the son of Hezron, the son of Perez,

the son of Judah, [34] the son of Jacob,

the son of Isaac, the son of Abraham,

the son of Terah, the son of Nahor,

[35] the son of Serug, the son of Reu,

the son of Peleg, the son of Eber,

the son of Shelah, [36] the son of Cainan,

the son of Arphaxad, the son of Shem,
the son of Noah, the son of Lamech,
[37] the son of Methuselah, the son of Enoch,
the son of Jared, the son of Mahalalel,
the son of Kenan, [38] the son of Enosh,
the son of Seth, the son of Adam,
   the son of God.

*1. How does Luke handle the event of Jesus' baptism?*

*2. What happened at Jesus' baptism?*

*3. What happened at our baptism, as you understand it?*

### DAY FIVE READING AND QUESTIONS:

Reread the entire passage (3:1-38).

*1. What do you think caused the crowds to go into the wilderness to be baptized by John?*

*2. How was Jesus to be different from John, according to John?*

*3. Why do you think Luke provided a genealogy of Jesus? What does it show?*

## MEDITATION

The wilderness was important to Israel. It was a place to encounter God. It was the home of the great prophets. Luke reminds us that Isaiah identified the wilderness as the place where he who would prepare the way for the Lord would emerge. John's message to the crowds who flowed out of the cities to hear him was clear—he called for a repentance leading to baptism for the forgiveness of sins.

The contrast between John's and Jesus' baptism was not the nature of forgiveness but the role of the Holy Spirit. Forgiveness has always been God's to give. He can grant it as and when he chooses. John was preparing the way of the Lord by calling people to *repentance* - its intent and force demonstrated in baptism. This baptism, submitted to because of a genuine repentance, led to the divine action of forgiveness. That led to a significant change demonstrated by a particular kind of life.

A life of true repentance, John taught, called for giving what we have to those in need, whether it be clothing or food. For tax collectors it meant they should be honest and fair; for soldiers it meant they should be content with their wages and not extort money. What would repentance mean for you? For me? What fruit are we called to bear?

God never intended for salvation to be an excuse for us to live a life of self-indulgence. God grants forgiveness as a gift that allows us to change the direction of our lives. We submit to baptism in order to open ourselves to God. No longer focused on our self-serving world-view, no longer hoarding what life offers for ourselves, we live in such a way that all see a radical change in us.

The Holy Spirit descended on Jesus at his baptism and God voiced his love for his obedient son. The Holy Spirit descends on us when we submit our lives to God through baptism. He confers to us "sonship." He is well pleased with us. Will we live our lives under his direction? We must ask this question as we continue to consider the life and teachings of Jesus.

"Lord, as we bask in the mercy of your forgiveness, may we truly repent from our self-focused lives and turn to you for direction and purpose."

# TEMPTATION AND REJECTION
## (Luke 4:1-44)

### DAY ONE READING AND QUESTIONS:

[1] Jesus, full of the Holy Spirit, returned from the Jordan and was led by the Spirit in the desert, [2] where for forty days he was tempted by the devil. He ate nothing during those days, and at the end of them he was hungry.

[3] The devil said to him, "If you are the Son of God, tell this stone to become bread."

[4] Jesus answered, "It is written: 'Man does not live on bread alone.'"

[5] The devil led him up to a high place and showed him in an instant all the kingdoms of the world. [6] And he said to him, "I will give you all their authority and splendor, for it has been given to me, and I can give it to anyone I want to. [7] So if you worship me, it will all be yours."

[8] Jesus answered, "It is written: 'Worship the Lord your God and serve him only.'"

[9] The devil led him to Jerusalem and had him stand on the highest point of the temple. "If you are the Son of God," he said, "throw yourself down from here. [10] For it is written:

" 'He will command his angels concerning you
    to guard you carefully;
[11] they will lift you up in their hands,
    so that you will not strike your foot against a stone.'"

[12] Jesus answered, "It says: 'Do not put the Lord your God to the test.'"

<sup>13</sup> When the devil had finished all this tempting, he left him until an opportune time.

*1. Why did Jesus go into the wilderness?*

*2. What was the nature of each of the three temptations?*

*3. How does Satan tempt us in similar ways?*

## DAY TWO READING AND QUESTIONS:

<sup>14</sup> Jesus returned to Galilee in the power of the Spirit, and news about him spread through the whole countryside. <sup>15</sup> He taught in their synagogues, and everyone praised him.

<sup>16</sup> He went to Nazareth, where he had been brought up, and on the Sabbath day he went into the synagogue, as was his custom. And he stood up to read. <sup>17</sup> The scroll of the prophet Isaiah was handed to him. Unrolling it, he found the place where it is written:

<sup>18</sup> "The Spirit of the Lord is on me,

because he has anointed me

to preach good news to the poor.

He has sent me to proclaim freedom for the prisoners

and recovery of sight for the blind,

to release the oppressed,

<sup>19</sup> to proclaim the year of the Lord's favor."

<sup>20</sup> Then he rolled up the scroll, gave it back to the attendant and sat down. The eyes of everyone in the synagogue were fastened on him, <sup>21</sup> and he began by saying to them, "Today this scripture is fulfilled in your hearing."

<sup>22</sup> All spoke well of him and were amazed at the gracious words that came from his lips. "Isn't this Joseph's son?" they asked.

<sup>23</sup> Jesus said to them, "Surely you will quote this proverb to me: 'Physician, heal yourself! Do here in your hometown what we have heard that you did in Capernaum.' "

<sup>24</sup> "I tell you the truth," he continued, "no prophet is accepted in his hometown. <sup>25</sup> I assure you that there were many widows in Israel in Elijah's time, when the sky was shut for three and a half years and there was a severe famine throughout the land. <sup>26</sup> Yet Elijah was not sent to any of them, but to a widow in Zarephath in the region of Sidon. <sup>27</sup> And there were many in Israel with leprosy in the time of Elisha the prophet, yet not one of them was cleansed—only Naaman the Syrian."

<sup>28</sup> All the people in the synagogue were furious when they heard this. <sup>29</sup> They got up, drove him out of the town, and took him to the brow of the hill on which the town was built, in order to throw him down the cliff. <sup>30</sup> But he walked right through the crowd and went on his way.

1. *What was Jesus' custom on the Sabbath?*

2. *What was Jesus to do according to the prophecy in Isaiah?*

3. *What specifically caused the listeners to be angered? Are there teachings of Jesus, which at first angered you, that have since become a valuable part of your kingdom walk?*

## DAY THREE READING AND QUESTIONS:

<sup>31</sup> Then he went down to Capernaum, a town in Galilee, and on the Sabbath began to teach the people. <sup>32</sup> They were amazed at his teaching, because his message had authority.

<sup>33</sup> In the synagogue there was a man possessed by a demon, an

evil spirit. He cried out at the top of his voice, [34] "Ha! What do you want with us, Jesus of Nazareth? Have you come to destroy us? I know who you are—the Holy One of God!"

[35] "Be quiet!" Jesus said sternly. "Come out of him!" Then the demon threw the man down before them all and came out without injuring him.

[36] All the people were amazed and said to each other, "What is this teaching? With authority and power he gives orders to evil spirits and they come out!" [37] And the news about him spread throughout the surrounding area.

1. *What consistently astonished those who heard Jesus teach? Why do you think this was so?*

2. *Why do you think the demons often acknowledged Jesus as "the Holy One" or "One sent from God," etc.?*

3. *Do you believe that there is still authoritative power in the name of Jesus?*

## DAY FOUR READING AND QUESTIONS:

[38] Jesus left the synagogue and went to the home of Simon. Now Simon's mother-in-law was suffering from a high fever, and they asked Jesus to help her. [39] So he bent over her and rebuked the fever, and it left her. She got up at once and began to wait on them.

[40] When the sun was setting, the people brought to Jesus all who had various kinds of sickness, and laying his hands on each one, he healed them. [41] Moreover, demons came out of many people, shouting, "You are the Son of God!" But he rebuked them and would not allow them to speak, because they knew he was the Christ.

⁴² At daybreak Jesus went out to a solitary place. The people were looking for him and when they came to where he was, they tried to keep him from leaving them. ⁴³ But he said, "I must preach the good news of the kingdom of God to the other towns also, because that is why I was sent." ⁴⁴ And he kept on preaching in the synagogues of Judea.

1. *What did the demons do (again) for which Jesus rebuked them?*

2. *After an exciting and successful day, what did Jesus do in the early morning? What did He gain from this time alone with God?*

3. *Do you think it would be beneficial spend significant time alone with God before making major decisions? Do you do this? Why or why not?*

## DAY FIVE READING AND QUESTIONS:

Reread the entire passage (4:1-44).

1. *Do you or have you ever fasted? Why or why not?*

2. *What might we learn from fasting that would strengthen us against the temptations of Satan?*

3. *If Jesus was about preaching to the poor, giving sight, and releasing the oppressed, should we do the same? Why or why not?*

## MEDITATION

The three temptations used against Jesus continue to be basic tools of the deceiver in today's world. Why would it have been so bad for Jesus to feed himself in the desert? Was turning a rock to bread really a sin? The question here is more basic than the need for food when hungry. Ultimately, it is, "In whom will you place your trust?" Jesus was in the wilderness at the behest of the Holy Spirit. Would he break his fast based on his needs or would he trust in the provision of God? Surely, Luke wants us to compare Jesus to the children of Israel. They failed the wilderness test. Even with the provision of daily manna, they constantly whined. They had not learned that there is something greater than physical bread that feeds the soul. After forty days alone with God, Jesus knew that "one does not live by bread alone." Do we know this truth?

The second temptation was for Jesus to reign over the earth without suffering. Satan offered him the world in exchange for his soul. Jesus knew there was and is only one foundation for a life worth living—to worship God and serve only him. The implications of this teaching are vast! How many things does Satan offer us to distract us from that one thing which would give us life? He continues to offer authority and splendor, all we have to do is bow down to the altar of self-worship. Without realizing it, we have forfeited kingdom life. In some way, we need to express daily the profound response of Jesus: "Worship the Lord your God and serve him only."

Satan even used the scriptures themselves to tempt Jesus. "Test your theory of sonship, Jesus, jump into the arms of God. Jump from the high point of the temple. You know the Scriptures promise God will save you." In some ways, this seems to be a noble test of faith. Gideon did this with his fleece, right? Jesus' response is unequivocal. "Do not put the Lord to the test." A life of faithful sonship calls one to *choose* trust over doubt. The faithful Son lives in complete assurance of God's design for His life. There is no need for a test. Faith is a choice beyond the need for testing.

Almost immediately after returning from Galilee, Jesus' trust is put to the test. His own townspeople attempt to cast him down a cliff, but God spared his life. God vindicated Jesus' trust in him. What angered the people of Nazareth? It seems they were willing to allow Jesus to be the fulfillment of Isaiah's words concerning the year of the Lord's favor. It was his pronouncement of God's blessings to Gentiles as well as Jews that so deeply angered them.

This chapter ends with Jesus in solitude with God. After a period of great victory—a time of healing and casting out demons—the people of Capernaum beg Jesus to stay. But he would not be distracted from his purpose by Satan or his admirers. His work was to proclaim the kingdom of God to all in Judea. The story of the life of Jesus is a magnificent example of one living a focused life. Time alone with God has a tendency to do that.

"Dear God, may we be in constant conversation with you. Help us see the need to seek out times of quiet solitude in your presence."

# CALLING, HEALING, AND FASTING
## (Luke 5)

### Day One Reading and Questions:

¹ One day as Jesus was standing by the Lake of Gennesaret, with the people crowding around him and listening to the word of God, ² he saw at the water's edge two boats, left there by the fishermen, who were washing their nets. ³ He got into one of the boats, the one belonging to Simon, and asked him to put out a little from shore. Then he sat down and taught the people from the boat.

⁴ When he had finished speaking, he said to Simon, "Put out into deep water, and let down the nets for a catch."

⁵ Simon answered, "Master, we've worked hard all night and haven't caught anything. But because you say so, I will let down the nets."

⁶ When they had done so, they caught such a large number of fish that their nets began to break. ⁷ So they signaled their partners in the other boat to come and help them, and they came and filled both boats so full that they began to sink.

⁸ When Simon Peter saw this, he fell at Jesus' knees and said, "Go away from me, Lord; I am a sinful man!" ⁹ For he and all his companions were astonished at the catch of fish they had taken, ¹⁰ and so were James and John, the sons of Zebedee, Simon's partners.

Then Jesus said to Simon, "Don't be afraid; from now on you will catch men." ¹¹ So they pulled their boats up on shore, left everything and followed him.

*1. Why was Simon reluctant to cast out the nets as requested by Jesus?*

*2. What do you think Simon was thinking about Jesus' understanding of his (Simon's) vocation of professional fisherman?*

*3. Do you believe that Jesus understands the nature of your vocation? Do you think this is important? Why or why not?*

## DAY TWO READING AND QUESTIONS:

[12] While Jesus was in one of the towns, a man came along who was covered with leprosy. When he saw Jesus, he fell with his face to the ground and begged him, "Lord, if you are willing, you can make me clean."

[13] Jesus reached out his hand and touched the man. "I am willing," he said. "Be clean!" And immediately the leprosy left him.

[14] Then Jesus ordered him, "Don't tell anyone, but go, show yourself to the priest and offer the sacrifices that Moses commanded for your cleansing, as a testimony to them."

[15] Yet the news about him spread all the more, so that crowds of people came to hear him and to be healed of their sicknesses. [16] But Jesus often withdrew to lonely places and prayed.

[17] One day as he was teaching, Pharisees and teachers of the law, who had come from every village of Galilee and from Judea and Jerusalem, were sitting there. And the power of the Lord was present for him to heal the sick. [18] Some men came carrying a paralytic on a mat and tried to take him into the house to lay him before Jesus. [19] When they could not find a way to do this because of the crowd, they went up on the roof and lowered him on his mat through the tiles into the middle of the crowd, right in front of Jesus.

[20] When Jesus saw their faith, he said, "Friend, your sins are forgiven."

²¹ The Pharisees and the teachers of the law began thinking to themselves, "Who is this fellow who speaks blasphemy? Who can forgive sins but God alone?"

²² Jesus knew what they were thinking and asked, "Why are you thinking these things in your hearts? ²³ Which is easier: to say, 'Your sins are forgiven,' or to say, 'Get up and walk'? ²⁴ But that you may know that the Son of Man has authority on earth to forgive sins. . . ." He said to the paralyzed man, "I tell you, get up, take your mat and go home." ²⁵ Immediately he stood up in front of them, took what he had been lying on and went home praising God. ²⁶ Everyone was amazed and gave praise to God. They were filled with awe and said, "We have seen remarkable things today."

1. *What do you find surprising of Jesus' treatment of the man stricken with leprosy?*

2. *What drove the friends of the paralyzed man to get their friend in front of Jesus?*

3. *Do we have the faith to seek Jesus in order to heal our difficulties or to bring our friends before him for healing (whether physical or other)? Why or why not?*

## DAY THREE READING AND QUESTIONS:

²⁷ After this, Jesus went out and saw a tax collector by the name of Levi sitting at his tax booth. "Follow me," Jesus said to him, ²⁸ and Levi got up, left everything and followed him.

²⁹ Then Levi held a great banquet for Jesus at his house, and a large crowd of tax collectors and others were eating with them. ³⁰ But the Pharisees and the teachers of the law who belonged to their sect

complained to his disciples, "Why do you eat and drink with tax collectors and 'sinners'?"

[31] Jesus answered them, "It is not the healthy who need a doctor, but the sick. [32] I have not come to call the righteous, but sinners to repentance."

*1. Why is it surprising that Jesus chose Levi as a disciple?*

*2. Do you find it disturbing or surprising that Jesus would go to Levi's party, especially considering the guests were "sinners and tax collectors"?*

*3. Do we see ourselves as sick or healthy? Are we need in need of a physician? Do we live a life manifesting our constant and desperate need of Jesus?*

## DAY FOUR READING AND QUESTIONS:

[33] They said to him, "John's disciples often fast and pray, and so do the disciples of the Pharisees, but yours go on eating and drinking."

[34] Jesus answered, "Can you make the guests of the bridegroom fast while he is with them? [35] But the time will come when the bridegroom will be taken from them; in those days they will fast."

[36] He told them this parable: "No one tears a patch from a new garment and sews it on an old one. If he does, he will have torn the new garment, and the patch from the new will not match the old. [37] And no one pours new wine into old wineskins. If he does, the new wine will burst the skins, the wine will run out and the wineskins will be ruined. [38] No, new wine must be poured into new wineskins. [39] And no one after drinking old wine wants the new, for he says, 'The old is better.' "

*1. Why didn't Jesus' disciples fast?*

2. *According to Jesus, would His disciples fast at some point? When?*

3. *Should we fast? If so, why? If not, why?*

### Day Five Reading and Questions:

Reread the entire passage (5:1-39).

1. *What have you learned about kingdom life from your vocation? If Peter was to become a "catcher of people" instead of fish, what would Jesus call you to become?*

2. *Is there anything in your life that does not belong that you **have not** taken to Jesus for healing? If so, intentionally take it to the Lord and pray for deliverance.*

3. *Have you found some teachings of Jesus to be incompatible with your present life? If so, will you trust him enough to allow him to change your life?*

## MEDITATION

It is important to let Jesus meet us in our places of work. This is where Jesus called Peter, James, and John to follow him. He calls us to walk intentionally with him daily, doing what he bids, right where we are. He will make each of us "catchers of souls." Do not fear, the "fish" come at his calling, not through our expertise. They came in places and times we would never expect. All we have to do is "lower the nets." Give Simon Peter credit for doing what Jesus said, even though he knew it was a waste of time. Unexpected blessings wait for those who trust Jesus knows more about their work than they do.

Is there anything or anyone Jesus cannot heal? He touched the untouchable, healed those beyond healing, and called those who had no hope to follow him. All who came to him in faith or responded to his call were healed. Not only were they healed, their lives were fully restored. The leper was cleansed, the paralytic even given the ability to walk away, carrying his mat! Will you trust Jesus to heal the deepest of your wounds? It is important that we not read and dismiss these events as irrelevant historical antiques to simply observe. These stories demonstrate to us how Jesus works in the lives of those who are hurting and who come to him in faith.

No matter where you are or where you've been, if you are willing to repent, Jesus calls you to follow him. All we have to do is admit that we are sick, and the gentle healer comes and does his work. Is it not amazing and enlightening that Levi threw Jesus a party after Jesus called him to be a disciple? Levi knew a reason to celebrate when he saw it! Without hesitation, Jesus went and rejoiced with Levi and his friends. Those at the party would make most of us very uncomfortable. They were, after all, notorious sinners. It was these, however, that Jesus sought. They knew they needed healing, and that is where a physician does his best work.

The life to which Jesus calls us simply does not fit into our world of self-comfort and self-focus. If we are to follow him, we will need a new container for this way of life. Old ways of thinking cannot be reformed—they must be transformed. The warning sign posted at the invitation to follow Jesus is, "Caution: heart bursting zone." Old hearts burst when trying to contend with the dynamic teachings of the kingdom. Here is the good news: the next sign posted is, "Rejoice: new hearts are freely given to those willing to follow Jesus."

"Lord, we bring our broken lives to you. Heal us. Grant us a new heart. Thank you for calling us to follow you."

# THE QUESTION OF GOD'S HEART

## (Luke 6:1-26)

### DAY ONE READING AND QUESTIONS:

[1] One Sabbath Jesus was going through the grainfields, and his disciples began to pick some heads of grain, rub them in their hands and eat the kernels. [2] Some of the Pharisees asked, "Why are you doing what is unlawful on the Sabbath?"

[3] Jesus answered them, "Have you never read what David did when he and his companions were hungry? [4] He entered the house of God, and taking the consecrated bread, he ate what is lawful only for priests to eat. And he also gave some to his companions." [5] Then Jesus said to them, "The Son of Man is Lord of the Sabbath."

1. *What did the Pharisees consider unlawful in the behavior of Jesus' disciples?*

2. *Why do you think Jesus responded with a story instead of a direct answer?*

3. *What do you think Jesus meant when He said, "The Son of Man is Lord of the Sabbath?"*

### DAY TWO READING AND QUESTIONS:

[6] On another Sabbath he went into the synagogue and was teaching, and a man was there whose right hand was shriveled. [7] The

Pharisees and the teachers of the law were looking for a reason to accuse Jesus, so they watched him closely to see if he would heal on the Sabbath. [8] But Jesus knew what they were thinking and said to the man with the shriveled hand, "Get up and stand in front of everyone." So he got up and stood there.

[9] Then Jesus said to them, "I ask you, which is lawful on the Sabbath: to do good or to do evil, to save life or to destroy it?"

[10] He looked around at them all, and then said to the man, "Stretch out your hand." He did so, and his hand was completely restored. [11] But they were furious and began to discuss with one another what they might do to Jesus.

1. *What were the Pharisees looking for in this situation? Did they have concern for the man with the withered hand?*

2. *Why did Jesus ask the question about doing good on the Sabbath?*

3. *What was the Pharisees' response to the wonderful demonstration of God's healing power? Why did they react as they did?*

## DAY THREE READING AND QUESTIONS:

[12] One of those days Jesus went out to a mountainside to pray, and spent the night praying to God. [13] When morning came, he called his disciples to him and chose twelve of them, whom he also designated apostles: [14] Simon (whom he named Peter), his brother Andrew, James, John, Philip, Bartholomew, [15] Matthew, Thomas, James son of Alphaeus, Simon who was called the Zealot, [16] Judas son of James, and Judas Iscariot, who became a traitor.

[17] He went down with them and stood on a level place. A large crowd of his disciples was there and a great number of people from

all over Judea, from Jerusalem, and from the coast of Tyre and Sidon, [18] who had come to hear him and to be healed of their diseases. Those troubled by evil spirits were cured, [19] and the people all tried to touch him, because power was coming from him and healing them all.

*1. What did Jesus do before He selected His disciples? For how long did He do this?*

*2. At this point in His ministry, who was coming to hear Jesus preach?*

*3. Have you ever prayed for more than a few minutes at a time? Why or why not?*

## Day Four Reading and Questions:

[20] Looking at his disciples, he said:
"Blessed are you who are poor,
   for yours is the kingdom of God.
[21] Blessed are you who hunger now,
   for you will be satisfied.
Blessed are you who weep now,
   for you will laugh.
[22] Blessed are you when men hate you,
   when they exclude you and insult you
   and reject your name as evil,
   because of the Son of Man.
[23] "Rejoice in that day and leap for joy, because great is your
   reward in heaven. For that is how their fathers treated the
   prophets.
[24] "But woe to you who are rich,
   for you have already received your comfort.

[25] Woe to you who are well fed now,
    for you will go hungry.
Woe to you who laugh now,
    for you will mourn and weep.
[26] Woe to you when all men speak well of you,
    for that is how their fathers treated the false prophets.

*1. Who is blessed according to Jesus? Why?*

*2. Who is in danger according to Jesus? Why?*

*3. Who are we in these passages? How do we apply these teachings to our lives?*

## Day Five Reading and Questions:

Reread the entire passage (6:1-26).

*1. Are there times when, out of fear of disobeying God's will, we have missed the point of God's law as did the Pharisees?*

*2. Why do you think the Pharisees tangled with Jesus so often concerning behavior on the Sabbath? Can you think of an issue in today's world that would be similar?*

*3. Why do you think Jesus said the poor are blessed and the rich are in trouble? How should we respond to this teaching?*

# MEDITATION

Do you ever wonder why Jesus doesn't just give a straight answer? Could he not have said, "Rubbing grain in your hand is not a violation of the Sabbath"? Jesus did not do this because he wanted to force his accusers to reconsider their overzealous interpretation of law. He reminded them of an episode involving one of their heroes—David. He obviously violated the law by eating the consecrated bread, yet was not condemned for it. Now one even greater than David was present. In fact, if they would see him for who he truly was, they would understand he was Lord of the Sabbath! This was an amazing claim. Jesus was not subject to the law, for he himself was the lawmaker.

We need to consider the whole issue of the Sabbath. It is one of the recurring points of conflict throughout the ministry of Jesus. The Pharisees were not evil. In fact, they were zealous for God's law. But they missed its point. They took God's gift to humanity of the Sabbath and made it a burden too heavy to bear. While the Sabbath may not be an issue for us, the matter of our understanding of God's law certainly is.

The second episode in this reading that the Sabbath question arises is deeply troubling. Here one is suffering because of a shriveled right hand. This was important in a culture that considered the left hand only worthy of unclean tasks. The Pharisees' concern for the law was heightened to the point that they were unmoved by the man's suffering. They only thing they saw in him was an opportunity to condemn Jesus. Even when Jesus showed mercy and performed one of his greatest healing miracles (can you imagine seeing a fully atrophied hand come to life?), all the Pharisees could see was an act of rebellion that must be silenced.

When our interpretation of law becomes our Lord, we are in trouble. God's commands are expressions of his love. They call us to righteous living. God has never been one to condemn for the failure to observe the fine points of law. He is, however, harshly condemning of those whose hearts are far from him. The Pharisees, in their desire to protect the law of God, sacrificed their relationship with him. Have we done the same with other issues of religious law? These events in the life of Jesus call us to introspection.

Once again, we see Jesus spending an entire night in prayer. He was about to choose his apostles. What other activity could possibly make sense? Jesus prayed because he knew his father would guide him. Do we pray with the same confidence? We cannot be like Jesus if we are not willing to follow his example in the discipline of prayer.

After choosing his disciples, Jesus began his "sermon on the plain." His opening words should trouble most of us. He once again proclaims his message of the great inversion. The poor and hungry are blessed. The rich and well-fed are warned. What does all this mean? Our world's values are dangerous and false. Those who acknowledge their needs will be satisfied; those without needs have already received their comfort. Will we open our minds and hearts to the precarious nature of our well-being?

"Lord of the Sabbath, teach us your ways. Keep us from false judgments, and open our eyes to the dangers of owning too much. May we be a blessing to the poor and hungry around us to your glory."

# LIFE'S TRUE FOUNDATION

### (Luke 6:27-49)

## Day One Reading and Questions:

[27] "But I tell you who hear me: Love your enemies, do good to those who hate you, [28] bless those who curse you, pray for those who mistreat you. [29] If someone strikes you on one cheek, turn to him the other also. If someone takes your cloak, do not stop him from taking your tunic. [30] Give to everyone who asks you, and if anyone takes what belongs to you, do not demand it back. [31] Do to others as you would have them do to you.

*1. To what action and emotion does Jesus call us in the treatment of our enemies? Do we do this? Why or why not?*

*2. Why should we turn the other cheek, or give more to those who take things from us? Do we do this? Why or why not?*

*3. What is the context of the "golden rule" in Luke? Do we practice the "golden rule"? Why or why not?*

## Day Two Reading and Questions:

[32] "If you love those who love you, what credit is that to you? Even 'sinners' love those who love them. [33] And if you do good to those who

are good to you, what credit is that to you? Even 'sinners' do that. [34] And if you lend to those from whom you expect repayment, what credit is that to you? Even 'sinners' lend to 'sinners,' expecting to be repaid in full. [35] But love your enemies, do good to them, and lend to them without expecting to get anything back. Then your reward will be great, and you will be sons of the Most High, because he is kind to the ungrateful and wicked. [36] Be merciful, just as your Father is merciful.

1. *Is it reasonable to think we could actually behave in this way? Why or why not?*

2. *What does all of this have to do with mercy, and how God is merciful in this way?*

3. *Do we manifest the character of God in our interaction with others? Why or why not?*

## DAY THREE READING AND QUESTIONS:

[37] "Do not judge, and you will not be judged. Do not condemn, and you will not be condemned. Forgive, and you will be forgiven. [38] Give, and it will be given to you. A good measure, pressed down, shaken together and running over, will be poured into your lap. For with the measure you use, it will be measured to you."

[39] He also told them this parable: "Can a blind man lead a blind man? Will they not both fall into a pit? [40] A student is not above his teacher, but everyone who is fully trained will be like his teacher.

[41] "Why do you look at the speck of sawdust in your brother's eye and pay no attention to the plank in your own eye? [42] How can you say to your brother, 'Brother, let me take the speck out of your eye,' when you yourself fail to see the plank in your own eye? You hypocrite, first

take the plank out of your eye, and then you will see clearly to remove the speck from your brother's eye.

*1. Why are we not to judge? Why are we, instead, to forgive?*

*2. To what extent are we to give? Do we do this? Why or why not?*

*3. What is the definition of a "disciple" in this passage?*

## DAY FOUR READING AND QUESTIONS:

[43] "No good tree bears bad fruit, nor does a bad tree bear good fruit. [44] Each tree is recognized by its own fruit. People do not pick figs from thornbushes, or grapes from briers. [45] The good man brings good things out of the good stored up in his heart, and the evil man brings evil things out of the evil stored up in his heart. For out of the overflow of his heart his mouth speaks.

[46] "Why do you call me, 'Lord, Lord,' and do not do what I say? [47] I will show you what he is like who comes to me and hears my words and puts them into practice. [48] He is like a man building a house, who dug down deep and laid the foundation on rock. When a flood came, the torrent struck that house but could not shake it, because it was well built. [49] But the one who hears my words and does not put them into practice is like a man who built a house on the ground without a foundation. The moment the torrent struck that house, it collapsed and its destruction was complete.

*1. The words that we speak do not originate in our mouths—from where to they come?*

*2. What would Jesus prefer we do than just call out "Lord, Lord"?*

3. *Are you tired of "why or why not" questions? The real question in this week's study is, "Do I believe the words of Jesus enough to do them? If we choose not to, to what are we compared?"*

## Day Five Reading and Questions:

Reread the entire passage (6:27-49).

1. *How is "loving your enemies" participating in the character of God?*

2. *What is the log in our eye that we should remove before attempting to help others?*

3. *What fruit from your life shows the world the goodness of your God-focused heart?*

## MEDITATION

What are we to do with teachings that call us to love our enemies, bless those who curse us, and give more than one forcefully takes from us - and not ask for it back? If we only practice love, giving, and doing good in a reciprocal relationship, then how are we different from anyone else? These teachings call us to a whole new kind of behavior - behavior which indicates one is tuned to God's heart instead of the cultural context of this world.

Jesus invites us to a better life. We have been freed from the emptiness of self-worship. We are free to be concerned for "the other," even if they are involved in wrongful behavior. Why love one's enemy? Why give to one who forcefully takes? Why do good to one who is doing you harm? The answer is: "Be merciful, just as your Father is merciful." We do them because they are reflections of God's character. When we love our enemies, we imitate God. Remember? While we were still enemies, he gave his only Son to die for us (Romans 5 and others). When we give more than requested, it reflects God's abundant giving. And how many times a day do we slap God with our ungodly behavior, while he just keeps loving us and turning the other cheek? If God responded to our affronts to him as we respond to those who do not give us the honor we think we deserve, none of us would have a chance.

These are difficult teachings. In order to do these things, we must have a deep faith in Jesus and who he claimed to be. If he is Son of God, the one through whom God created all, then Jesus knows how we ought to live. Someone—or perhaps several people—influence all of us deeply. We are their disciple, perhaps without knowing it. Will we choose Jesus as the one we should intentionally imitate? It depends on how we regard him. Too many of us are like the blind led by the blind—we follow them into the pit. Jesus calls us to follow him and learn the true meaning of life. Can we develop the wisdom to intentionally walk with him on a daily basis?

If we did so, we would lose our desire to judge, and instead be intent on helping others. We would become by nature that which would naturally produce good rather than evil. But such good cannot occur outside of authentic discipleship. Only when Jesus rules our hearts will we conform to his teaching. It is not enough just to hear the words of Jesus, or even to understand them. They must become a part of who we are. Otherwise, when the storms of life hit—and they will—our lives will not stand.

"Lord, give us the wisdom to acknowledge your teachings are true. Give us the strength and courage to live according to your will. May those around us feast on the good fruit of a life focused on you."

# THE KEY TO KINGDOM JOY

## (Luke 7:1-50)

### DAY ONE READING AND QUESTIONS:

¹ When Jesus had finished saying all this in the hearing of the people, he entered Capernaum. ² There a centurion's servant, whom his master valued highly, was sick and about to die. ³ The centurion heard of Jesus and sent some elders of the Jews to him, asking him to come and heal his servant. ⁴ When they came to Jesus, they pleaded earnestly with him, "This man deserves to have you do this, ⁵ because he loves our nation and has built our synagogue." ⁶ So Jesus went with them.

He was not far from the house when the centurion sent friends to say to him: "Lord, don't trouble yourself, for I do not deserve to have you come under my roof. ⁷ That is why I did not even consider myself worthy to come to you. But say the word, and my servant will be healed. ⁸ For I myself am a man under authority, with soldiers under me. I tell this one, 'Go,' and he goes; and that one, 'Come,' and he comes. I say to my servant, 'Do this,' and he does it."

⁹ When Jesus heard this, he was amazed at him, and turning to the crowd following him, he said, "I tell you, I have not found such great faith even in Israel." ¹⁰ Then the men who had been sent returned to the house and found the servant well

*1. Why do you think the centurion sent Jewish elders to ask Jesus to heal his slave?*

*2. What did the centurion mean when he said he, too, was a man of authority? What did that have to do with Jesus?*

*3. What was unusual about the centurion's request and why did Jesus marvel at it?*

## DAY TWO READING AND QUESTIONS:

[11] Soon afterward, Jesus went to a town called Nain, and his disciples and a large crowd went along with him. [12] As he approached the town gate, a dead person was being carried out—the only son of his mother, and she was a widow. And a large crowd from the town was with her. [13] When the Lord saw her, his heart went out to her and he said, "Don't cry."

[14] Then he went up and touched the coffin, and those carrying it stood still. He said, "Young man, I say to you, get up!" [15] The dead man sat up and began to talk, and Jesus gave him back to his mother.

[16] They were all filled with awe and praised God. "A great prophet has appeared among us," they said. "God has come to help his people." [17] This news about Jesus spread throughout Judea and the surrounding country.

*1. What caused Jesus to respond to the widow in her sorrow?*

*2. After Jesus raised the man from the dead, what does the text say he did with him?*

*3. What insight do we gain about Jesus in this incident, and how can we become like Him in this?*

## DAY THREE READING AND QUESTIONS:

[18] John's disciples told him about all these things. Calling two of them, [19] he sent them to the Lord to ask, "Are you the one who was to come, or should we expect someone else?"

[20] When the men came to Jesus, they said, "John the Baptist sent us to you to ask, 'Are you the one who was to come, or should we expect someone else?' "

[21] At that very time Jesus cured many who had diseases, sicknesses and evil spirits, and gave sight to many who were blind. [22] So he replied to the messengers, "Go back and report to John what you have seen and heard: The blind receive sight, the lame walk, those who have leprosy are cured, the deaf hear, the dead are raised, and the good news is preached to the poor. [23] Blessed is the man who does not fall away on account of me."

[24] After John's messengers left, Jesus began to speak to the crowd about John: "What did you go out into the desert to see? A reed swayed by the wind? [25] If not, what did you go out to see? A man dressed in fine clothes? No, those who wear expensive clothes and indulge in luxury are in palaces. [26] But what did you go out to see? A prophet? Yes, I tell you, and more than a prophet. [27] This is the one about whom it is written:

" 'I will send my messenger ahead of you, who will prepare your way before you.'

[28] I tell you, among those born of women there is no one greater than John; yet the one who is least in the kingdom of God is greater than he."

[29] (All the people, even the tax collectors, when they heard Jesus' words, acknowledged that God's way was right, because they had been baptized by John. [30] But the Pharisees and experts in the law rejected God's purpose for themselves, because they had not been baptized by John.)

³¹ "To what, then, can I compare the people of this generation? What are they like? ³² They are like children sitting in the marketplace and calling out to each other:

" 'We played the flute for you,
> and you did not dance;
> we sang a dirge,
> and you did not cry.'

³³ For John the Baptist came neither eating bread nor drinking wine, and you say, 'He has a demon.' ³⁴ The Son of Man came eating and drinking, and you say, 'Here is a glutton and a drunkard, a friend of tax collectors and "sinners." ' ³⁵ But wisdom is proved right by all her children."

*1. What was John's question? Why do you think he asked this?*

*2. What was Jesus' appraisal of John and his work?*

*3. What is the relationship of John's ministry with that of Jesus and how should this affect us?*

## Day Four Reading and Questions:

³⁶ Now one of the Pharisees invited Jesus to have dinner with him, so he went to the Pharisee's house and reclined at the table. ³⁷ When a woman who had lived a sinful life in that town learned that Jesus was eating at the Pharisee's house, she brought an alabaster jar of perfume, ³⁸ and as she stood behind him at his feet weeping, she began to wet his feet with her tears. Then she wiped them with her hair, kissed them and poured perfume on them.

³⁹ When the Pharisee who had invited him saw this, he said to himself, "If this man were a prophet, he would know who is touching

him and what kind of woman she is—that she is a sinner."

[40] Jesus answered him, "Simon, I have something to tell you."

"Tell me, teacher," he said.

[41] "Two men owed money to a certain moneylender. One owed him five hundred denarii, and the other fifty. [42] Neither of them had the money to pay him back, so he canceled the debts of both. Now which of them will love him more?"

[43] Simon replied, "I suppose the one who had the bigger debt canceled."

"You have judged correctly," Jesus said.

[44] Then he turned toward the woman and said to Simon, "Do you see this woman? I came into your house. You did not give me any water for my feet, but she wet my feet with her tears and wiped them with her hair. [45] You did not give me a kiss, but this woman, from the time I entered, has not stopped kissing my feet. [46] You did not put oil on my head, but she has poured perfume on my feet. [47] Therefore, I tell you, her many sins have been forgiven—for she loved much. But he who has been forgiven little loves little."

[48] Then Jesus said to her, "Your sins are forgiven."

[49] The other guests began to say among themselves, "Who is this who even forgives sins?"

[50] Jesus said to the woman, "Your faith has saved you; go in peace

*1. How did Simon, the Pharisee, let Jesus know he did not "measure up"?*

*2. What do you find surprising about the behavior of the sinful woman?*

*3. Do you think there are really those who need to be forgiven less? What is the point of this story for us?*

## Day Five Reading and Questions:

Reread the entire passage (7:1-50).

1. *How could we manifest the kind of faith in Jesus shown by the centurion?*

2. *How can we develop hearts of compassion that would emulate Jesus?*

3. *How did the sinful woman know she would find forgiveness at his feet? Are we approachable by sinners as was Jesus? What can we do to cultivate this?*

# MEDITATION

Faith is found in unusual places! Of all people, a Roman centurion amazes Jesus with his faith. While the religious leaders around Jesus cannot figure out who Jesus is, this soldier knows. Granted, he has an unusually kind and loving heart towards the Jews and his servant, but it is his lack of religious baggage that allows him to see clearly the authority of God in Jesus. Do we have such faith?

How about compassion? This is another wonderful attribute of Jesus. The widow of Nain had no hope—her livelihood was gone. She had no husband and now no son. Jesus' heart went out to her, Luke tells us. How do we respond to the broken hearted around us? It is significant that Luke notes Jesus, after bringing the son to life, "gave him back to his mother." Jesus was constantly giving and invites us to a life of similar compassion and generosity.

What do we do with the question of John about Jesus? Not even John could understand what Jesus was doing. While he preached in the wilderness and called for repentance, Jesus taught in the cities and went to parties. John wanted to know if Jesus was truly Messiah. Jesus told John's disciples to tell John what they had seen. Clearly this was the inbreaking of the kingdom of God! The lame were walking, the blind could see again, the dead are raised—who but God could do such things! With John, we are encouraged by these marvelous signs of the kingdom.

But then Jesus calls us to consider John's part in God's plan. He was different from Jesus. From the wilderness he called for repentance and baptism to new life. Jesus, instead, demonstrated the joy of living in the kingdom. But both "cues" of the kingdom were missed. Like children playing a game of interpreting actions, they misunderstood the need for repentance leading to joy! True repentance is the key to kingdom joy. Without repentance, there is not new life. And so the sinful woman breaks every social convention and falls at the feet of Jesus. Overjoyed by the forgiveness she has found, she sobs tears of joy while the cynical Pharisee sees only a pathetic sinner and false prophet. Oh, how blind are those who refuse to see!

The Pharisees could not understand the kingdom of God for they had nothing of which to repent, at least in their own eyes. They would not subject themselves to baptism, because they did not need a new beginning. They were fine just like they were. How tragic! To be in the presence of the prince of life and refuse to hear his healing message. Will we journey to the wilderness and repent, that times of refreshing may come? Wisdom, after all, is proved right by all her children. Ironic, is it not? It was the forgiven women who was a child of wisdom. Simon never got it. He played the fool.

"Gracious and compassionate Lord, lead us to the desert of repentance, that we might find the joy of your kingdom!"

# OF PARABLES AND POWER
### (Luke 8)

## DAY ONE READING AND QUESTIONS:

[1] After this, Jesus traveled about from one town and village to another, proclaiming the good news of the kingdom of God. The Twelve were with him, [2] and also some women who had been cured of evil spirits and diseases: Mary (called Magdalene) from whom seven demons had come out; [3] Joanna the wife of Cuza, the manager of Herod's household; Susanna; and many others. These women were helping to support them out of their own means.

[4] While a large crowd was gathering and people were coming to Jesus from town after town, he told this parable: [5] "A farmer went out to sow his seed. As he was scattering the seed, some fell along the path; it was trampled on, and the birds of the air ate it up. [6] Some fell on rock, and when it came up, the plants withered because they had no moisture. [7] Other seed fell among thorns, which grew up with it and choked the plants. [8] Still other seed fell on good soil. It came up and yielded a crop, a hundred times more than was sown."

When he said this, he called out, "He who has ears to hear, let him hear."

[9] His disciples asked him what this parable meant. [10] He said, "The knowledge of the secrets of the kingdom of God has been given to you, but to others I speak in parables, so that,

" 'though seeing, they may not see;
though hearing, they may not understand.'

[11] "This is the meaning of the parable: The seed is the word of God. [12] Those along the path are the ones who hear, and then the devil comes and takes away the word from their hearts, so that they may not believe and be saved. [13] Those on the rock are the ones who receive the word with joy when they hear it, but they have no root. They believe for a while, but in the time of testing they fall away. [14] The seed that fell among thorns stands for those who hear, but as they go on their way they are choked by life's worries, riches and pleasures, and they do not mature. [15] But the seed on good soil stands for those with a noble and good heart, who hear the word, retain it, and by persevering produce a crop.

*1. What was the content of Jesus' preaching?*

*2. Why do you think Luke includes the information about the women following Jesus?*

*3. What are parables and why do you think Jesus used them?*

## Day Two Reading and Questions:

[16] "No one lights a lamp and hides it in a jar or puts it under a bed. Instead, he puts it on a stand, so that those who come in can see the light. [17] For there is nothing hidden that will not be disclosed, and nothing concealed that will not be known or brought out into the open. [18] Therefore consider carefully how you listen. Whoever has will be given more; whoever does not have, even what he thinks he has will be taken from him."

[19] Now Jesus' mother and brothers came to see him, but they were not able to get near him because of the crowd. [20] Someone told him, "Your mother and brothers are standing outside, wanting to see you."

[21] He replied, "My mother and brothers are those who hear God's word and put it into practice."

<sup>22</sup> One day Jesus said to his disciples, "Let's go over to the other side of the lake." So they got into a boat and set out. <sup>23</sup> As they sailed, he fell asleep. A squall came down on the lake, so that the boat was being swamped, and they were in great danger.

<sup>24</sup> The disciples went and woke him, saying, "Master, Master, we're going to drown!"

He got up and rebuked the wind and the raging waters; the storm subsided, and all was calm. <sup>25</sup> "Where is your faith?" he asked his disciples.

In fear and amazement they asked one another, "Who is this? He commands even the winds and the water, and they obey him."

*1. What is Jesus teaching in his illustration of the lamp?*

*2. How do Jesus' words about his true kindred impact you? Are you his brother by this definition?*

*3. Were the disciples justified in their fear of the storm? Why or why not?*

## Day Three Reading and Questions:

<sup>26</sup> They sailed to the region of the Gerasenes, which is across the lake from Galilee. <sup>27</sup> When Jesus stepped ashore, he was met by a demon-possessed man from the town. For a long time this man had not worn clothes or lived in a house, but had lived in the tombs. <sup>28</sup> When he saw Jesus, he cried out and fell at his feet, shouting at the top of his voice, "What do you want with me, Jesus, Son of the Most High God? I beg you, don't torture me!" <sup>29</sup> For Jesus had commanded the evil spirit to come out of the man. Many times it had seized him, and though he was chained hand and foot and kept under guard, he had broken his chains and had been driven by the demon into solitary places.

<sup>30</sup> Jesus asked him, "What is your name?"

"Legion," he replied, because many demons had gone into him. [31] And they begged him repeatedly not to order them to go into the Abyss.

[32] A large herd of pigs was feeding there on the hillside. The demons begged Jesus to let them go into them, and he gave them permission. [33] When the demons came out of the man, they went into the pigs, and the herd rushed down the steep bank into the lake and was drowned.

[34] When those tending the pigs saw what had happened, they ran off and reported this in the town and countryside, [35] and the people went out to see what had happened. When they came to Jesus, they found the man from whom the demons had gone out, sitting at Jesus' feet, dressed and in his right mind; and they were afraid. [36] Those who had seen it told the people how the demon-possessed man had been cured. [37] Then all the people of the region of the Gerasenes asked Jesus to leave them, because they were overcome with fear. So he got into the boat and left.

[38] The man from whom the demons had gone out begged to go with him, but Jesus sent him away, saying, [39] "Return home and tell how much God has done for you." So the man went away and told all over town how much Jesus had done for him.

1. *Why were the demons able to see Jesus for who he truly was?*

2. *Why do you think the demons, when released into the pigs, hurled themselves into the sea?*

3. *Who is the first commissioned evangelist in Luke?*

## DAY FOUR READING AND QUESTIONS:

[40] Now when Jesus returned, a crowd welcomed him, for they were all expecting him. [41] Then a man named Jairus, a ruler of the syna-

gogue, came and fell at Jesus' feet, pleading with him to come to his house [42] because his only daughter, a girl of about twelve, was dying.

As Jesus was on his way, the crowds almost crushed him. [43] And a woman was there who had been subject to bleeding for twelve years, but no one could heal her. [44] She came up behind him and touched the edge of his cloak, and immediately her bleeding stopped.

[45] "Who touched me?" Jesus asked.

When they all denied it, Peter said, "Master, the people are crowding and pressing against you."

[46] But Jesus said, "Someone touched me; I know that power has gone out from me."

[47] Then the woman, seeing that she could not go unnoticed, came trembling and fell at his feet. In the presence of all the people, she told why she had touched him and how she had been instantly healed. [48] Then he said to her, "Daughter, your faith has healed you. Go in peace."

[49] While Jesus was still speaking, someone came from the house of Jairus, the synagogue ruler. "Your daughter is dead," he said. "Don't bother the teacher any more."

[50] Hearing this, Jesus said to Jairus, "Don't be afraid; just believe, and she will be healed."

[51] When he arrived at the house of Jairus, he did not let anyone go in with him except Peter, John and James, and the child's father and mother. [52] Meanwhile, all the people were wailing and mourning for her. "Stop wailing," Jesus said. "She is not dead but asleep."

[53] They laughed at him, knowing that she was dead. [54] But he took her by the hand and said, "My child, get up!" [55] Her spirit returned, and at once she stood up. Then Jesus told them to give her something to eat. [56] Her parents were astonished, but he ordered them not to tell anyone what had happened.

*1. Why do you think Jesus stopped the crowd to identify the woman "who had touched" him?*

*2. What made the woman well according to Jesus?*

*3. What do you think Jesus was saying when he commented that the girl was not dead, but only sleeping? Might he be reflecting on his view that physical death is not the real problem?*

### Day Five Reading and Questions:

Reread the entire passage (8:1-56).

*1. What type of soil would you be in the parable of the sower? Why?*

*2. Imagine being at sea and experiencing Jesus calming the storm. How do you think you would have reacted?*

*3. Whom did Jesus first commission as an evangelist in Luke? Why do you think Jesus told him to go and tell what had happened to him when Jesus told others not to do so?*

# MEDITATION

If you were Theophilus, by this point in Luke's story you have to wonder what is going on. Jesus' actions up to this point have made it abundantly clear that he is Messiah. Yet some not only refused to believe, they openly opposed Jesus.

Jesus answers our dilemma with one of the best known parables—that of the sower. In Jesus' day, a farmer would scatter seed by hand. Jesus might have been pointing to a sower as he recounted his parable. The point of this parable is clear—the power of the seed is undeniable. But the effect of the seed is not dependent on its own power, but the readiness of the soil to accept it. In good soil it was amazingly productive—ten times as powerful as the best harvest possible. But not all the ground is ready to receive the seed. It is amazing how relevant this parable is to our times, isn't it? We still have those who hear the word of God, even accept it, but quickly leave their faith when life doesn't go their way. Or others who allow the worries of life to choke out their faith and allow the weeds to destroy the good their lives might have been. There are also still good hearts who receive the word and produce wonderful fruit for the kingdom. Which soil would you be?

Parables were not used to conceal the message but to illuminate willing hearts concerning the nature of the kingdom of God. Hardened hearts, however, were incapable of understanding. The "seeing they may not see and hearing they may not understand" passage referred to those who were unwilling to submit to God.

This reading ends with four miracles that demonstrate the amazing power of Jesus. In the first, Jesus calms a storm at sea with a simple rebuke. In the second, he ordered a legion of demons to leave a man. Called to heal an important man's daughter, he stopped on the way to heal a suffering woman. During the delay caused by the women, the little girl died. So Jesus proceeded to raise her back to life! What was there that Jesus could not do? The world had never seen such amazing power. Yet many still refused to believe. How about you and me? Do we believe Jesus did these things? If so, is there anything we could not take to him for healing? He has power over nature, over a legion of demons, and over death itself. Will our hearts willingly receive the word and produce a harvest of witness of his love and power?

"All-powerful Lord, cultivate the soil of my life that I may receive the seed of your word with gladness and produce a hundred fold harvest, bringing glory to you."

# THE KINGDOM MISSION

## (Luke 9:1-27)

### Day One Reading and Questions:

¹ When Jesus had called the Twelve together, he gave them power and authority to drive out all demons and to cure diseases, ² and he sent them out to preach the kingdom of God and to heal the sick. ³ He told them: "Take nothing for the journey—no staff, no bag, no bread, no money, no extra tunic. ⁴ Whatever house you enter, stay there until you leave that town. ⁵ If people do not welcome you, shake the dust off your feet when you leave their town, as a testimony against them." ⁶ So they set out and went from village to village, preaching the gospel and healing people everywhere.

  *1. What did Jesus give the apostles as He sent them out?*

  *2. What were they to proclaim?*

  *3. What stipulations did Jesus give the twelve before He sent them out?*

### Day Two Reading and Questions:

⁷ Now Herod the tetrarch heard about all that was going on. And he was perplexed, because some were saying that John had been raised from the dead, ⁸ others that Elijah had appeared, and still others that

one of the prophets of long ago had come back to life. [9] But Herod said, "I beheaded John. Who, then, is this I hear such things about?" And he tried to see him.

*1. What perplexed Herod?*

*2. Why do you think Luke included this small paragraph in this point of the story?*

*3. For what does this question of Herod prepare us? When will he finally see Jesus?*

## DAY THREE READING AND QUESTIONS:

[10] When the apostles returned, they reported to Jesus what they had done. Then he took them with him and they withdrew by themselves to a town called Bethsaida, [11] but the crowds learned about it and followed him. He welcomed them and spoke to them about the kingdom of God, and healed those who needed healing.

[12] Late in the afternoon the Twelve came to him and said, "Send the crowd away so they can go to the surrounding villages and countryside and find food and lodging, because we are in a remote place here."

[13] He replied, "You give them something to eat."

They answered, "We have only five loaves of bread and two fish—unless we go and buy food for all this crowd." [14] (About five thousand men were there.)

But he said to his disciples, "Have them sit down in groups of about fifty each." [15] The disciples did so, and everybody sat down. [16] Taking the five loaves and the two fish and looking up to heaven, he gave thanks and broke them. Then he gave them to the disciples to set before the people. ¹⁷ They all ate and were satisfied, and the disciples picked up twelve basketfuls of broken pieces that were left over.

1. *What is Jesus' reaction to the crowds who continued to follow Him, even when He tried to get away? Why did He feel the way He did about the crowds?*

2. *By the apostles' question to Jesus, do you get the idea their response to the crowds continually following them was different from that of Jesus? Why?*

3. *Why do you think Jesus asked his apostles to give the crowd something to eat?*

## DAY FOUR READING AND QUESTIONS:

¹⁸ Once when Jesus was praying in private and his disciples were with him, he asked them, "Who do the crowds say I am?"

¹⁹ They replied, "Some say John the Baptist; others say Elijah; and still others, that one of the prophets of long ago has come back to life."

²⁰ "But what about you?" he asked. "Who do you say I am?"

Peter answered, "The Christ of God."

²¹ Jesus strictly warned them not to tell this to anyone. ²² And he said, "The Son of Man must suffer many things and be rejected by the elders, chief priests and teachers of the law, and he must be killed and on the third day be raised to life."

²³ Then he said to them all: "If anyone would come after me, he must deny himself and take up his cross daily and follow me. ²⁴ For whoever wants to save his life will lose it, but whoever loses his life for me will save it. ²⁵ What good is it for a man to gain the whole world, and yet lose or forfeit his very self? ²⁶ If anyone is ashamed of me and

my words, the Son of Man will be ashamed of him when he comes in his glory and in the glory of the Father and of the holy angels. [27] I tell you the truth, some who are standing here will not taste death before they see the kingdom of God."

*1. Why did Jesus ask the apostles what the crowds were thinking?*

*2. What was Peter's response to Jesus' question about who He was?*

*3. Why did Jesus immediately follow Peter's confession with a pronouncement of His own death?*

### DAY FIVE READING AND QUESTIONS:

Reread the entire passage (9:1-27).

*1. Do Jesus' instructions to the twelve, as he sent them out, apply to us? If so, how?*

*2. Do we ever limit what Jesus can do through us by measuring our response to a need by our own resources and abilities? What can we do to get beyond this type of thinking?*

*3. What must we do daily if we want to follow Jesus? Have we done this? Do we continually do this? Why is this a requirement for authentic discipleship?*

# MEDITATION

The sending out of the twelve is their first opportunity to put into action what they've learned. Jesus sends them out on a journey of faith. In a sense, it is a first tasting for the disciples of the reality of living in the kingdom of God. They would need nothing. God would provide. Off they went, casting out demons, healing the sick, and proclaiming the good news of the kingdom of God.

This mission caused such commotion that word came all the way to Herod. He was disturbed, wanting to know what all this was about and who Jesus was. It is in this context that Luke tells us of Jesus feeding the five thousand with five loaves of bread and two fish. The answer is clear to Herod's question—Jesus was Messiah. One of the long-standing expectations of Messiah was that he would feed his people miraculously and abundantly.

So, when Jesus (while praying—don't miss how often Luke points this out) asked his disciples who the crowds thought he was, the answer should have been "Messiah." But the crowds were not convinced. For them, Jesus was something less—maybe because the title of Messiah was too precious to give without undeniable confir-mation. But what did the disciples think? In Peter's answer, "The Christ of God" we reach the first plot climax of Luke's gospel. The Christ, indeed! Why would Jesus immediately warn them not to tell anyone who he was? Had he not just sent them out to proclaim the good news of the kingdom of God?

At this point that we must slowly digest the teachings of Jesus. We have arrived at this moment in Luke to begin to allow Jesus to teach us the true nature of kingdom life. He was Messiah, but not the one everyone expected. It might even be possible that for many who claim faith in him, he is not who they expect him to be. Being Messiah did not mean freeing Israel from Roman rule. It was so much more! Yet it would require the unthinkable. Messiah would have to die. And the news gets worse. His followers, his true followers, have to die as well. If they do not die, they will never find life.

This is the heart of discipleship. There is no way to overempha-size the importance of this reading. Read 9:18-27 often. Ask yourself,

"Do I believe this is true?" We know it to be true because we know the rest of the story. But do we live it? Daily?

"Jesus, we acknowledge with all of our hearts that you are the Messiah, the anointed of God! Help us remember what it means to be your followers. May we deny ourselves and pick up our crosses daily, so that we might follow you and find true life!"

# THE TRANSFIGURATION
## (Luke 9:28-45)

### DAY ONE READING AND QUESTIONS:

²⁸ About eight days after Jesus said this, he took Peter, John and James with him and went up onto a mountain to pray. ²⁹ As he was praying, the appearance of his face changed, and his clothes became as bright as a flash of lightning. ³⁰ Two men, Moses and Elijah, ³¹ appeared in glorious splendor, talking with Jesus. They spoke about his departure, which he was about to bring to fulfillment at Jerusalem.

1. *Why do you think Jesus just took Peter, James and John with him up the mountain?*

2. *What happened while Jesus was praying?*

3. *Why do think it is significant that Moses and Elijah appeared with Jesus? What were they discussing?*

### DAY TWO READING AND QUESTIONS:

³² Peter and his companions were very sleepy, but when they became fully awake, they saw his glory and the two men standing with him. ³³ As the men were leaving Jesus, Peter said to him, "Master, it is good for us to be here. Let us put up three shelters—one for you, one

for Moses and one for Elijah." (He did not know what he was saying.)

[34] While he was speaking, a cloud appeared and enveloped them, and they were afraid as they entered the cloud. [35] A voice came from the cloud, saying, "This is my Son, whom I have chosen; listen to him." [36] When the voice had spoken, they found that Jesus was alone. The disciples kept this to themselves, and told no one at that time what they had seen.

*1. What were the three apostles doing while Jesus prayed?*

*2. What did the three see?*

*3. What was Peter's reaction, and why do you think he responded this way?*

## DAY THREE READING AND QUESTIONS:

[37] The next day, when they came down from the mountain, a large crowd met him. [38] A man in the crowd called out, "Teacher, I beg you to look at my son, for he is my only child. [39] A spirit seizes him and he suddenly screams; it throws him into convulsions so that he foams at the mouth. It scarcely ever leaves him and is destroying him. [40] I begged your disciples to drive it out, but they could not."

[41] "O unbelieving and perverse generation,"Jesus replied, "how long shall I stay with you and put up with you? Bring your son here."

[42] Even while the boy was coming, the demon threw him to the ground in a convulsion. But Jesus rebuked the evil spirit, healed the boy and gave him back to his father. [43] And they were all amazed at the greatness of God.

    *1. What problem did Jesus encounter as he came down the mountain to the rest of the apostles?*

    *2. What was Jesus' response?*

    *3. What does this event teach us about our abilities to present effectively God's kingdom to those around us?*

## Day Four Reading and Questions:

While everyone was marveling at all that Jesus did, he said to his disciples, ⁴⁴ "Listen carefully to what I am about to tell you: The Son of Man is going to be betrayed into the hands of men." ⁴⁵ But they did not understand what this meant. It was hidden from them, so that they did not grasp it, and they were afraid to ask him about it.

    *1. Why do you think Jesus reintroduced the topic of his betrayal?*

    *2. Why was this teaching so difficult for the disciples?*

    *3. Why do you think they were afraid to ask Jesus for clarification on this matter?*

## Day Five Reading and Questions:

Reread the entire passage (9:28-45).

    *1. Imagine for a moment what it will be like to see Jesus in his glory. Write a brief description of what we might see on that great day.*

*2. What does Jesus' response to the inability of his disciples to cast out the demon tell us about what caused their lack of power?*

*3. What might we avoid in the teachings of Jesus? It is possible we have ignored major points of his teaching because they are not what we want to hear?*

## MEDITATION

Why was Jesus going up onto a mountain? Oh, yes, to pray. Taking his closest friends with him, Jesus wanted to spend time thinking and praying about what was about to happen. This was a time of great trial in his life. In one of the most majestic scenes in Jesus' life, while in prayer he was transformed into his glory, with Moses and Elijah appearing with him. They spoke together of the wonderful plan of God—but it involved great pain on Jesus' behalf. They discussed the ultimate exodus, of God leading his people out of the slavery of sin! Peter did not know what to say. But his heart was doubtlessly filled with fear and great joy. After all, who else had actually seen Moses and Elijah—considered the greatest heroes of Israel's story? Likely, Peter thought the kingdom of God had come! Here was the realization of the hope of Israel. So, let's build them a dwelling place, that from this mountain the kingdom might be established. Instead, a cloud appeared and enveloped them. This was not an ordinary cloud, or it would not have elicited fear. This was the presence of God, and he spoke to them words we need to hear "This is my Son, whom I have chosen, listen to him."

This is an amazing moment. It speaks of the majesty of God, and it tells us of his deep love for his Son. Why did this happen? In response to the prayers of Jesus, the loving Father assured his Son through conversation with Moses and Elijah that what was about to occur in Jerusalem was God's plan from the beginning. God himself affirms to us that Jesus is the culmination of all that he has revealed to us. It is him we must hear and obey.

We are well aware of the failure of Jesus' disciples at the base of the mountain. Lacking faith, they were not able to cast a demon out of a young boy. Jesus quickly dispatched the demon, then turned to his disciples to remind them what was about to occur in Jerusalem. Their minds were so confused by their own expectations they could not hear what Jesus was saying. In fact, it was so confusing to them, they did not even have the courage to ask Jesus what he meant. Might their confusion be attributed to their lack of time in prayer? After all, it was there that Jesus found his conviction to do the will of the Father.

"Loving Father, teach us to pray as Jesus prayed. Teach us the importance of time alone with you. May the cloud of our confusion dissolve as we enter the glorious cloud of your presence."

# TRUE GREATNESS
## (Luke 9:46-61)

### Day One Reading and Questions:

⁴⁶ An argument started among the disciples as to which of them would be the greatest. ⁴⁷ Jesus, knowing their thoughts, took a little child and had him stand beside him. ⁴⁸ Then he said to them, "Whoever welcomes this little child in my name welcomes me; and whoever welcomes me welcomes the one who sent me. For he who is least among you all—he is the greatest."

1. *Why do you think the disciples were arguing over who was the greatest disciple?*

2. *Why would Jesus use a child to answer their questions concerning greatness?*

3. *What did Jesus mean when he said, "The least among all of you is the greatest?"*

### Day Two Reading and Questions:

⁴⁹ "Master," said John, "we saw a man driving out demons in your name and we tried to stop him, because he is not one of us."
⁵⁰ "Do not stop him," Jesus said, "for whoever is not against you is for you."

*1. What was the man doing that disturbed the disciples?*

*2. Why did they tell him to stop?*

*3. Did Jesus agree with their behavior?*

## Day Three Reading and Questions:

[51] As the time approached for him to be taken up to heaven, Jesus resolutely set out for Jerusalem. [52] And he sent messengers on ahead, who went into a Samaritan village to get things ready for him; [53] but the people there did not welcome him, because he was heading for Jerusalem. [54] When the disciples James and John saw this, they asked, "Lord, do you want us to call fire down from heaven to destroy them?" [55] But Jesus turned and rebuked them, [56] and they went to another village.

*1. What do you think the messengers going ahead of Jesus did for Him in preparing for His arrival?*

*2. Why didn't the Samaritans receive Jesus?*

*3. What was the reaction of James and John to the people of the village? Why did Jesus rebuke them?*

## Day Four Reading and Questions:

[57] As they were walking along the road, a man said to him, "I will follow you wherever you go."
[58] Jesus replied, "Foxes have holes and birds of the air have nests, but the Son of Man has no place to lay his head."

[59] He said to another man, "Follow me."

But the man replied, "Lord, first let me go and bury my father."

[60] Jesus said to him, "Let the dead bury their own dead, but you go and proclaim the kingdom of God."

[61] Still another said, "I will follow you, Lord; but first let me go back and say good-by to my family."

[62] Jesus replied, "No one who puts his hand to the plow and looks back is fit for service in the kingdom of God."

*1. What is Jesus calling for in these verses?*

*2. Why would Jesus not want someone to bury his father?*

*3. What did Jesus mean when He said we should not look back or we are not fit for the kingdom of God?*

## DAY FIVE READING AND QUESTIONS:

Reread the entire passage (9:46-62).

*1. Do you believe that the least are the greatest in the kingdom? Why or why not?*

*2. What are we willing to sacrifice in order to follow Jesus? Have we made it too easy to follow Jesus in our churches?*

*3. What do you think Jesus would say to us in our culture about the nature of the undivided loyalty needed to participate fully in the kingdom?*

# MEDITATION

Since he first spoke of his impending death, Jesus has been dealing with misconceptions concerning the kingdom of God. In a sense, it is the "good news, bad news" kind of announcement. Ultimately, it is all good news, but it is going to take some ripping away of old ways of thinking before we will be able to understand. That's the bad news. All that we have invested in this world to show that we are important and great is worthless. As difficult as it is to believe, we manifest the image of God more in loving a child than in being a "great leader" of men from the world's point of view. Will we believe Jesus in this?

Our desire for worldly greatness often interferes with what God wants to do to make us *truly* great. Do you remember the apostles' inability to cast out a demon? In this reading they encountered someone who was able to do what they could not, even though he was not one of them. Why? Apparently, he was using the name of Jesus in faith, and having success. They, in their search for greatness, had forgotten that the power was not in them. The power was and is in the name of Jesus, spoken in faith. In whose power do we trust?

We have made following Jesus as Lord much too easy. We may regard as overly harsh Jesus' response to one who said he was ready to follow Jesus anywhere. Nevertheless, this is the level of commitment to which he calls each of us. There is simply nothing in this world that is worth enough to distract us from our purpose of glorifying God. In just a few days, Jesus would embody that truth. He would die a miserable death to show us this profound truth. Therefore, he "resolutely set out for Jerusalem." What about us? What directs our lives? What causes us to get out of bed in the morning? Are we intentionally and resolutely walking with Jesus towards Jerusalem?

"Loving Jesus, thank you for your example of unwavering faith. Teach us how to walk with unyielding devotion toward that for which

God created each of us. May we learn from you how to turn away from the distractions of this world and focus on God's purpose for our lives."

# SATAN FALLS!

## (Luke 10:1-24)

### DAY ONE READING AND QUESTIONS:

¹ After this the Lord appointed seventy-two others and sent them two by two ahead of him to every town and place where he was about to go. ² He told them, "The harvest is plentiful, but the workers are few. Ask the Lord of the harvest, therefore, to send out workers into his harvest field. ³ Go! I am sending you out like lambs among wolves. ⁴ Do not take a purse or bag or sandals; and do not greet anyone on the road.

⁵ "When you enter a house, first say, 'Peace to this house.' ⁶ If a man of peace is there, your peace will rest on him; if not, it will return to you. ⁷ Stay in that house, eating and drinking whatever they give you, for the worker deserves his wages. Do not move around from house to house.

⁸ "When you enter a town and are welcomed, eat what is set before you. ⁹ Heal the sick who are there and tell them, 'The kingdom of God is near you.' ¹⁰ But when you enter a town and are not welcomed, go into its streets and say, ¹¹ 'Even the dust of your town that sticks to our feet we wipe off against you. Yet be sure of this: The kingdom of God is near.' ¹² I tell you, it will be more bearable on that day for Sodom than for that town.

*1. Why did Jesus send out the seventy-two?*

*2. What were his instructions? How are they similar to those he gave the twelve in 9:1-6?*

*3. What was to be their message?*

## Day Two Reading and Questions:

¹³ "Woe to you, Korazin! Woe to you, Bethsaida! For if the miracles that were performed in you had been performed in Tyre and Sidon, they would have repented long ago, sitting in sackcloth and ashes. ¹⁴ But it will be more bearable for Tyre and Sidon at the judgment than for you. ¹⁵ And you, Capernaum, will you be lifted up to the skies? No, you will go down to the depths.

¹⁶ "He who listens to you listens to me; he who rejects you rejects me; but he who rejects me rejects him who sent me."

*1. Why did Jesus pronounce "woes" against cities?*

*2. What was the ultimate message Jesus wanted these cities to hear?*

*3. What does Jesus' instruction concerning "listening to them" (disciples) and its relationship to "listening to me" (Jesus) tell us about our work in announcing the kingdom?*

## Day Three Reading and Questions:

¹⁷ The seventy-two returned with joy and said, "Lord, even the demons submit to us in your name."

¹⁸ He replied, "I saw Satan fall like lightning from heaven. ¹⁹ I have given you authority to trample on snakes and scorpions and to overcome

all the power of the enemy; nothing will harm you. [20] However, do not rejoice that the spirits submit to you, but rejoice that your names are written in heaven."

*1. What were the seventy-two excited about as they returned?*

*2. What did Jesus see? What do you think this means?*

*3. For what should they and we ultimately rejoice? Why?*

## Day Four Reading and Questions:

[21] At that time Jesus, full of joy through the Holy Spirit, said, "I praise you, Father, Lord of heaven and earth, because you have hidden these things from the wise and learned, and revealed them to little children. Yes, Father, for this was your good pleasure.

[22] "All things have been committed to me by my Father. No one knows who the Son is except the Father, and no one knows who the Father is except the Son and those to whom the Son chooses to reveal him."

[23] Then he turned to his disciples and said privately, "Blessed are the eyes that see what you see. [24] For I tell you that many prophets and kings wanted to see what you see but did not see it, and to hear what you hear but did not hear it."

*1. Why does Luke constantly mention the Holy Spirit?*

*2. Can we have the same kind of joy experienced here by Jesus? Why or why not? If so, how?*

*3. Why were the disciples blessed in a special way? Are we so blessed?*

## Day Five Reading and Questions:

Reread the entire passage (10:1-24).

> *1. How might the instructions to the seventy-two apply to us?*

> *2. Do we have power through the name of Jesus? If so, what is it?*

> *3. Have we seen and heard the message for which the disciples were pronounced "blessed"? Do we regard the truth of the kingdom of God in this way?*

# MEDITATION

Luke wants to stir our hearts about the urgency of spreading the kingdom message. So many need to hear the good news; so many have had their hearts prepared by God. He seeks them and makes the harvest ready, but so few are willing to reap the harvest! Luke wants us to embrace the call of the seventy-two. We are to entrust ourselves to the abundant provisions of God. Jesus calls us to embody his ministry, as lambs sent out among wolves.

The urgency of the message is made clear by the strong condemnation of those who would not accept it. Jesus pronounces woes over the unrepentant cities because they have rejected him by rejecting those he sent. If we are about the Lord's work, wherever we are, its success does not depend on our ability to perform. The power is in the message. If those who hear it turn it down, they are not rejecting us, but God himself.

The return of the seventy-two is exciting! Kingdom work in the lost world had begun, with demons falling before the powerful name of Jesus, who saw the fall of Satan himself. Was this simply a metaphorical statement—or a true vision? It doesn't really matter. Jesus' statement is one of kingdom purpose. When the armies of God war against Satan's power in the name of Jesus, Satan cannot stop the victorious march. God's reign is expanded; his will is being accomplished. However, it is not power being manifested over evil that is the real blessing. What is truly wonderful is that these individuals had their names written in God's book. Jesus' work was to return God's erring people to him, and while power over evil was exciting, the true test of the success of Jesus' coming was that these were submitting themselves to God's will. They were now living the kingdom life!

Jesus then celebrates. Turning to his disciples (and to us, as we participate in the story) he says, "You are truly blessed." The prophets of old and the great kings have all wanted to know what we know. Do we realize the incredible blessing of knowing the eternal will of God? In this dramatic moment, as Jesus anticipates his death but celebrates his victory over Satan, we stand next to God's faithful Son! What a position of privilege! The one who knows the very mind of God calls us to learn about life from Him. May we have ears to hear!

"Almighty God, give us the courage and strength to be your workers in the fields of harvest. May we battle Satan in the name of Jesus and bring joy to you as we glorify your name."

# KINGDOM NEIGHBORS
### (Luke 10:25-42)

## DAY ONE READING AND QUESTIONS:

[25] On one occasion an expert in the law stood up to test Jesus. "Teacher," he asked, "what must I do to inherit eternal life?"

[26] "What is written in the Law?" he replied. "How do you read it?"

[27] He answered: " 'Love the Lord your God with all your heart and with all your soul and with all your strength and with all your mind'; and, 'Love your neighbor as yourself.'"

[28] "You have answered correctly," Jesus replied. "Do this and you will live."

1. *What was the expert in the law's motivation for asking about "eternal life"?*

2. *Why do you think Jesus answered his question with a question?*

3. *What do you think Jesus meant by "do this and you will live?"*

## DAY TWO READING AND QUESTIONS:

[29] But he wanted to justify himself, so he asked Jesus, "And who is my neighbor?"

1. *Why did the expert of the law feel he had to justify himself?*

*2. Do you think the expert of the law had found the life he sought? Why or why not?*

*3. Can you think of a time when you were more interested in justifying yourself than discovering truth?*

## Day Three Reading and Questions:

[30] In reply Jesus said: "A man was going down from Jerusalem to Jericho, when he fell into the hands of robbers. They stripped him of his clothes, beat him and went away, leaving him half dead. [31] A priest happened to be going down the same road, and when he saw the man, he passed by on the other side. [32] So too, a Levite, when he came to the place and saw him, passed by on the other side. [33] But a Samaritan, as he traveled, came where the man was; and when he saw him, he took pity on him. [34] He went to him and bandaged his wounds, pouring on oil and wine. Then he put the man on his own donkey, took him to an inn and took care of him. [35] The next day he took out two silver coins and gave them to the innkeeper. 'Look after him,' he said, 'and when I return, I will reimburse you for any extra expense you may have.'

[36] "Which of these three do you think was a neighbor to the man who fell into the hands of robbers?"

[37] The expert in the law replied, "The one who had mercy on him." Jesus told him, "Go and do likewise."

*1. Why do you think Jesus answered the lawyer's question with a story?*

*2. Why didn't Jesus begin his story by saying, "Let me tell you the story of the good Samaritan"?*

*3. What question did Jesus really answer?*

## Day Four Reading and Questions:

[38] As Jesus and his disciples were on their way, he came to a village where a woman named Martha opened her home to him. [39] She had a sister called Mary, who sat at the Lord's feet listening to what he said. [40] But Martha was distracted by all the preparations that had to be made. She came to him and asked, "Lord, don't you care that my sister has left me to do the work by myself? Tell her to help me!"

[41] "Martha, Martha," the Lord answered, "you are worried and upset about many things, [42] but only one thing is needed. Mary has chosen what is better, and it will not be taken away from her."

*1. Why is it surprising that Mary sat at Jesus' feet to learn from him?*

*2. What distracted Martha from hearing Jesus' teaching?*

*3. What is the "one thing" of which Jesus spoke?*

## Day Five Reading and Questions:

Reread the entire passage (10:25-42).

*1. If we would ask Jesus, "What is the key to a meaningful life", what do you think his answer to us would be?*

*2. In what sense are we each of the characters in the story of the Good Samaritan? The priest or Levite? The one beaten and robbed? The Good Samaritan?*

*3. What most often distracts you from that which is truly important?*

# MEDITATION

I am "the expert in the law" in this story. That is why I designed
this reading to give you only one verse on day two. Too often, I have
gone to Jesus in order to justify my behavior instead of seeking the life
he offers. How about you? How do you approach the biblical text? Do
you ask all the questions, or do you allow the story of Jesus interrogate
you? This was the real problem of the "Bible experts" of Jesus' day.
The desire to justify themselves absolutely consumed them. They had
developed elaborate systems of protecting the laws they deemed most
important, only to miss the most obvious one—submitting oneself
fully to God.

The question asked by the expert in the law is not what most of
us think it was. He was not asking how to live after death. He was
asking how one finds the life of eternal significance offered
throughout the Old Testament (see Deuteronomy 4-6 for the promise
of "life" attached to observing the Law) to those who are obedient.
Jesus asked him what was in the Law—and more importantly, "How
do you read it?" What a great question! How do we read God's word?
Well, it turns out that the expert already knew the answer to Jesus'
question—he knew the major commands. When Jesus acknowledged
he was right, he was embarrassed. If he already knew, then why did he
ask? Now he shows us how he read the text. In order to justify himself,
he asked, "Who is the neighbor I am instructed to love?" Jesus did not
give him the answer he wanted.

Jesus masterfully constructs a shocking story. One is traveling on
a dangerous road and is robbed, beaten, and left half-dead. We all
know this story well. Who will help this man? Not the priest or the
Levite. They had other things to do. Along comes a Samaritan. I
would guess that most listening to Jesus were convinced the
Samaritan would finish the dying man off. That's what Samaritans

did, in the opinion of the Jews. But no, this Samaritan shows extravagant mercy. He heard the cries of pain and went well beyond what the most gracious among them would do to bring the unfortunate man to health. How does this story answer the expert's question? It does not. It reframes the question so that a more valid one is asked. In the kingdom, in the true life sought by all, one does not ask "to whom must I show love?" The question is, "To whom will I be a neighbor?" We will find the life which we all seek only when our hearts feel and our minds think in the ways of our heavenly Father. Are we not all the man beaten, robbed, and left to die? Has God not responded to us with extravagant mercy? So, Jesus says, "Go and do likewise, and you will find the life you seek."

But the spiritual life is not complete with serving alone. There are times when we need to sit at the feet of Jesus and soak in his teaching. Martha found herself fully absorbed in the world of tasks, and even accused Jesus of not caring about all she had to do. Jesus lovingly chided her for being distracted by many things and missing the only thing needed. What might that one thing be? Surely he was speaking of seeking for and living in the kingdom of God. In that place, there is no frantic activity to prove one's worth through extravagant hospitality. There is peace, joy, and love at the feet of Jesus. Where will you live?

"Gracious and merciful Lord, open my heart to your word. May I show your great love to all those I encounter who are in need. May I find peace and joy at your feet."

# LORD, TEACH US TO PRAY

## (Luke 11:1-13)

### Day One Reading and Questions:

¹ One day Jesus was praying in a certain place. When he finished, one of his disciples said to him, "Lord, teach us to pray, just as John taught his disciples."

² He said to them, "When you pray, say:

" 'Father,

hallowed be your name,

your kingdom come.

³ Give us each day our daily bread.

⁴ Forgive us our sins,

for we also forgive everyone who sins against us.

And lead us not into temptation.' "

*1. What had Jesus been doing when the disciples asked him to teach them to pray?*

*2. What do you think might have been the difference between the way John the Baptist taught his disciples to pray and how Jesus prayed?*

*3. What do you find most surprising about "The Lord's Prayer"?*

## Day Two Reading and Questions:

[5] Then he said to them, "Suppose one of you has a friend, and he goes to him at midnight and says, 'Friend, lend me three loaves of bread, [6] because a friend of mine on a journey has come to me, and I have nothing to set before him.'

[7] "Then the one inside answers, 'Don't bother me. The door is already locked, and my children are with me in bed. I can't get up and give you anything.' [8] I tell you, though he will not get up and give him the bread because he is his friend, yet because of the man's boldness he will get up and give him as much as he needs.

*1. Why would a man ask another for bread late in the evening?*

*2. What do you think these verses teach us about prayer?*

*3. Are you persistent in your prayers?*

## Day Three Reading and Questions:

[9] "So I say to you: Ask and it will be given to you; seek and you will find; knock and the door will be opened to you. [10] For everyone who asks receives; he who seeks finds; and to him who knocks, the door will be opened."

*1. Why is it important to ask?*

*2. For what do you think Jesus is encouraging us to search?*

*3. What is the door at which we are to knock?*

## Day Four Reading and Questions:

[11] "Which of you fathers, if your son asks for a fish, will give him a snake instead? [12] Or if he asks for an egg, will give him a scorpion? [13] If you then, though you are evil, know how to give good gifts to your children, how much more will your Father in heaven give the Holy Spirit to those who ask him!"

1. *What was Jesus telling his disciples about God's response to prayer with his example of a fish and snake?*

2. *Why would Jesus call us "evil"?*

3. *Why did Jesus tell us God would give us His Holy Spirit as an illustration of God's gracious response to our requests in prayer?*

## Day Five Reading and Questions:

Reread the entire passage (11:1-13).

1. *What do you think Luke wants us to learn from the prayer life of Jesus?*

2. *What does this prayer teach us about our relationship with God?*

3. *How confident are you that God responds to your prayers? How can we build each other's faith in the power of prayer?*

# MEDITATION

When Jesus came back from times of prayer, his apostles could tell a difference. So much so, in fact, that they wanted to learn to pray as he prayed. By this point in Luke's gospel, surely we, too, would like to know more about how Jesus prayed. What is there about this prayer that is so significant? The words themselves have been repeated countless times throughout the history of the Christian faith. Have they made a difference? Certainly. Especially if we understand the profound focus of the prayer. Its main point? It is a change of address. If the words are spoken from a heart fully entrenched in the matters of this world, the prayer means nothing. But if it is the expression of a heart firmly committed to living in God's kingdom—it is a powerful expression of a philosophy of life. Jesus is calling us to live where he lives—in the loving care of God.

Through Jesus Christ, we celebrate our adoption as children by addressing God in prayer as our Father. We then express the purpose of our lives in him. If his name is to be hallowed, he will accomplish this through our faithful obedience to his will (Ezekiel 36:23). His name is holy, but we make it visibly holy in the world when we live a holy life. In this way, God's kingdom comes to our world in ever-increasing ways. If this is our life, then our petition is for God to care for our daily needs, as he has promised to do. We have no need to worry over this—we depend on our Father to provide. As we live in his gracious mercy and forgiveness, we, too, forgive. What else could we possibly do? Then we acknowledge our frail nature and ask God to protect us as he guides us. Note that the presupposition to that final phrase, "lead us not into temptation" is that God does lead us. We ask that he be mindful of our weakness and our need for his care.

Jesus moves from specific petitions of prayer into an explanation of why we should be confident in prayer. Even a friend not wanting to be inconvenienced will respond to the need of another if one is persistent. How much more confident should we be of God's loving response to us, for our prayers are never an inconvenience? Thus, we should have the confidence to boldly ask, seek, and knock—for God is always ready to respond. Jesus may offend us by calling us "evil," yet knowing how to give good gifts. But when comparing us to God, what other word is appropriate? If we who are evil know how to give good things, how much more does God, who gives us his Holy Spirit? Luke reminds us God has already given us his ultimate gift—his very Spirit. How could we ever doubt that he will give us exactly what we need? Such is life in the kingdom of God! From what address (location) do you offer your prayers to God?

"Father, hallowed by your name, your kingdom come. Give us each day our daily bread. Forgive us our sins, for we also forgive everyone who sins against us. And lead us not into temptation."

# THE KINGDOM PERSPECTIVE

### (Luke 11:14-36)

## DAY ONE READING AND QUESTIONS:

[14] Jesus was driving out a demon that was mute. When the demon left, the man who had been mute spoke, and the crowd was amazed. [15] But some of them said, "By Beelzebub, the prince of demons, he is driving out demons." [16] Others tested him by asking for a sign from heaven.

[17] Jesus knew their thoughts and said to them: "Any kingdom divided against itself will be ruined, and a house divided against itself will fall. [18] If Satan is divided against himself, how can his kingdom stand? I say this because you claim that I drive out demons by Beelzebub. [19] Now if I drive out demons by Beelzebub, by whom do your followers drive them out? So then, they will be your judges. [20] But if I drive out demons by the finger of God, then the kingdom of God has come to you.

[21] "When a strong man, fully armed, guards his own house, his possessions are safe. [22] But when someone stronger attacks and overpowers him, he takes away the armor in which the man trusted and divides up the spoils.

[23] "He who is not with me is against me, and he who does not gather with me, scatters.

1. *Why do you think some people accused Jesus of using Satan's power to cast out demons?*

*2. What was Jesus' response when accused of working by Satan's power?*

*3. According to Jesus, what has come if he was working by God's power?*

## DAY TWO READING AND QUESTIONS:

[24] "When an evil spirit comes out of a man, it goes through arid places seeking rest and does not find it. Then it says, 'I will return to the house I left.' [25] When it arrives, it finds the house swept clean and put in order. [26] Then it goes and takes seven other spirits more wicked than itself, and they go in and live there. And the final condition of that man is worse than the first."

[27] As Jesus was saying these things, a woman in the crowd called out, "Blessed is the mother who gave you birth and nursed you."

[28] He replied, "Blessed rather are those who hear the word of God and obey it."

*1. What was Jesus teaching about the nature of ridding oneself of an unclean spirit?*

*2. What does this passage teach us about our fight against sin?*

*3. What point was Jesus making by not accepting the woman's praise? What does this mean to us?*

## DAY THREE READING AND QUESTIONS:

[29] As the crowds increased, Jesus said, "This is a wicked genera-tion. It asks for a miraculous sign, but none will be given it except the sign of Jonah. [30] For as Jonah was a sign to the Ninevites, so also will

the Son of Man be to this generation. ³¹ The Queen of the South will rise at the judgment with the men of this generation and condemn them; for she came from the ends of the earth to listen to Solomon's wisdom, and now one greater than Solomon is here. ³² The men of Nineveh will stand up at the judgment with this generation and condemn it; for they repented at the preaching of Jonah, and now one greater than Jonah is here.

*1. Why was Jesus upset about people asking for a sign?*

*2. What was "the sign of Jonah"?*

*3. What is Jesus' warning in these verses? What does this mean to us?*

## Day Four Reading and Questions:

³³ "No one lights a lamp and puts it in a place where it will be hidden, or under a bowl. Instead he puts it on its stand, so that those who come in may see the light. ³⁴ Your eye is the lamp of your body. When your eyes are good, your whole body also is full of light. But when they are bad, your body also is full of darkness. ³⁵ See to it, then, that the light within you is not darkness. ³⁶ Therefore, if your whole body is full of light, and no part of it dark, it will be completely lighted, as when the light of a lamp shines on you."

*1. What do you think Jesus was saying in his discussion of a lamp and its purpose?*

*2. What do you think Jesus meant when he said: "The eye is the lamp of the body"?*

*3. How can our bodies be "full of light"?*

## Day Five Reading and Questions:

Reread the entire passage (11:14-36).

1. *Have you ever attributed something to Satan that you later found to be a work of God? If so, when and how did you change your thinking on the matter?*

2. *Why is it not enough just to "clean" our hearts of sin? What should we put in its place?*

3. *How would you describe your "worldview" (what you see) through the illumination of your eyes? Do you see what God sees?*

# MEDITATION

This lesson is entitled "The Kingdom Perspective" for a reason. The actions and teachings of Jesus make no sense when viewed from an earthly perspective (worldview). Salvation means God gives us the gift of seeing things and people as he sees them. Jesus came to give us new eyes. In Jesus' day, the eye was used to describe what we call worldview or ideology. The eyes illuminated the heart. How do your "eyes" see the world in which you live?

A flawed view of the world and of God is what allowed some to suggest Jesus was working by the power of Satan (Beelzebub). Can you imagine anyone thinking this way? Here was their problem—Jesus did not say what they wanted him to say. He did not do what they expected him to do, therefore, he could not be from God. In their own minds, there was no possibility that they might be the ones who were wrong. Consider: Jesus ate with sinners, walked with common people, chided the religious leaders about their view of the Law, and called people to greatness through servanthood, of all things! Because he did not say what they wanted to hear, they attributed his power to the evil one.

The solution? They continually asked for more signs so that they might believe. But what more could he do? Had he not healed the sick, given sight to the blind, allowed the paralyzed to walk, calmed the sea, fed the multitude, and raised the dead? Yes! But they needed more. Why? Their eyes filled their minds with darkness. They could not see because they refused to see.

God did not send his light into the world to hide it. He placed it on a stand for all to see. Unfortunately, there were those so blinded by their own expectations (flawed worldview or perspective), even the Light of the world looked like darkness (the work of Satan). How do you view your world? What do you see?

"Giver of light and life, open our eyes that we may see Jesus in the fullness of his brilliance. Grant us the joy of walking in his light."

# MISGUIDED RELIGION

## (Luke 11:37-12:12)

### Day One Reading and Questions:

[37] When Jesus had finished speaking, a Pharisee invited him to eat with him; so he went in and reclined at the table. [38] But the Pharisee, noticing that Jesus did not first wash before the meal, was surprised.

[39] Then the Lord said to him, "Now then, you Pharisees clean the outside of the cup and dish, but inside you are full of greed and wickedness. [40] You foolish people! Did not the one who made the outside make the inside also? [41] But give what is inside the dish to the poor, and everything will be clean for you.

[42] "Woe to you Pharisees, because you give God a tenth of your mint, rue and all other kinds of garden herbs, but you neglect justice and the love of God. You should have practiced the latter without leaving the former undone.

[43] "Woe to you Pharisees, because you love the most important seats in the synagogues and greetings in the marketplaces.

[44] "Woe to you, because you are like unmarked graves, which men walk over without knowing it."

*1. What surprised the Pharisees about Jesus' behavior? Why?*

*2. What did Jesus suggest was the proper methodology of cleaning?*

*3. What "woes" did Jesus pronounce against the Pharisees?*

## Day Two Reading and Questions:

⁴⁵ One of the experts in the law answered him, "Teacher, when you say these things, you insult us also."

⁴⁶ Jesus replied, "And you experts in the law, woe to you, because you load people down with burdens they can hardly carry, and you yourselves will not lift one finger to help them.

⁴⁷ "Woe to you, because you build tombs for the prophets, and it was your forefathers who killed them. ⁴⁸ So you testify that you approve of what your forefathers did; they killed the prophets, and you build their tombs. ⁴⁹ Because of this, God in his wisdom said, 'I will send them prophets and apostles, some of whom they will kill and others they will persecute.' ⁵⁰ Therefore this generation will be held responsible for the blood of all the prophets that has been shed since the beginning of the world, ⁵¹ from the blood of Abel to the blood of Zechariah, who was killed between the altar and the sanctuary. Yes, I tell you, this generation will be held responsible for it all.

⁵² "Woe to you experts in the law, because you have taken away the key to knowledge. You yourselves have not entered, and you have hindered those who were entering."

*1. Why were experts in the law offended by Jesus' words?*

*2. What were the sins that Jesus exposed?*

*3. What do you think is the "key to knowledge" of which Jesus spoke?*

## Day Three Reading and Questions:

¹¹:⁵³ When Jesus left there, the Pharisees and the teachers of the

law began to oppose him fiercely and to besiege him with questions, [54] waiting to catch him in something he might say.

[12:1] Meanwhile, when a crowd of many thousands had gathered, so that they were trampling on one another, Jesus began to speak first to his disciples, saying: "Be on your guard against the yeast of the Pharisees, which is hypocrisy. [2] There is nothing concealed that will not be disclosed, or hidden that will not be made known. [3] What you have said in the dark will be heard in the daylight, and what you have whispered in the ear in the inner rooms will be proclaimed from the roofs.

*1. Why do you think the scribes and Pharisees were so opposed to Jesus?*

*2. What was the "yeast of the Pharisees" of which Jesus warned his followers?*

*3. What do you think Jesus was teaching when he said, "Nothing covered will be left uncovered"? What should we do in light of this teaching?*

## DAY FOUR READING AND QUESTIONS:

[4] "I tell you, my friends, do not be afraid of those who kill the body and after that can do no more. [5] But I will show you whom you should fear: Fear him who, after the killing of the body, has power to throw you into hell. Yes, I tell you, fear him. [6] Are not five sparrows sold for two pennies ? Yet not one of them is forgotten by God. [7] Indeed, the very hairs of your head are all numbered. Don't be afraid; you are worth more than many sparrows.

[8] "I tell you, whoever acknowledges me before men, the Son of Man will also acknowledge him before the angels of God. [9] But he

who disowns me before men will be disowned before the angels of God. [10] And everyone who speaks a word against the Son of Man will be forgiven, but anyone who blasphemes against the Holy Spirit will not be forgiven.

[11] "When you are brought before synagogues, rulers and authorities, do not worry about how you will defend yourselves or what you will say, [12] for the Holy Spirit will teach you at that time what you should say."

1. *Who are we to fear? Who are we not to fear? Why?*

2. *What do we have to do with sparrows? What should this comparison teach us?*

3. *What do you think constitutes blaspheming the Holy Spirit? Does Jesus' teaching about the Holy Spirit in verse 12 have an application to us today? Why or why not?*

## DAY FIVE READING AND QUESTIONS:

Reread the entire passage (11:37-12:12).

1. *Make a list of modern day offenses that would be comparable to the sins of the Pharisees.*

2. *Make a list of modern day offences that would be comparable to the sins of the experts of the law.*

3. *How can we avoid these offences?*

# MEDITATION

The Pharisees and experts in the law were not evil men. They were thoroughly convinced they were defenders of God's truth. They were thoroughly wrong. Why does Luke include this list of woes against these religious leaders? It is not to vindicate Jesus—God took care of that in the resurrection! Luke wants to warn us of the dangers of misguided religious fever. It is important that we not read this passage in order to condemn the Pharisees and scribes, but to ask if these offenses might be applicable to us.

The Pharisee could not help but notice Jesus did not join him in his elaborate cleansing ritual before the meal. This was not just a matter of cleaning hands before eating: it was participating in a ritual that cleansed one of contamination from unwitting contact by a Gentile. Jesus responded to his host's disapproval with a new view of cleansing—starting from the inside. Scripture consistently teaches that no physical act can increase one's favor with God. Only those actions that come from the heart have meaning. Outward actions devoid of inward change have no meaning in the kingdom. The tragic irony was that the Pharisees were making people unclean by their emphasis on ritual, rather than leading them to God-honoring purity.

When we emphasize visible behavior over inward conversion, we are in serious trouble. It is much easier to be "religious" than it is to be "faithful." If we would allow the Spirit of God to do his work in cleansing our hearts, then appropriate actions of worship would follow. The experts in the law had taken away the possibility of kingdom life from those learning at their feet. How? Rather than entering God's kingdom (life submitted to God), they used knowledge as power, destroying not only their own lives, but of all who turned to them for understanding.

Are we death or are we life? The dreadful yeast of the Pharisees was their religion of self-promotion and hypocrisy. They were living out the sin of blasphemy against the Holy Spirit. Their rigid religious system prohibited the work of the Spirit in their lives. Such a condition leaves one without hope.

But here is the good news. If we will give our hearts to God and allow the Holy Spirit to do his work through us, we have no reason to fear. Even when we find ourselves in situations of great danger in the defense of our faith, the Spirit will give us the words to say. So, what will it be? Will we participate in a religion based on external behaviors, or will we submit to the guidance of the Holy Spirit? One is death; one is life. It is our choice.

"Gracious Lord, keep us from false religion. Make us mindful of empty actions that do not point our lives toward you. Teach us to yield to your Holy Spirit."

# IN WHAT WORLD WILL YOU LIVE?

### (Luke 12:13-59)

## DAY ONE READING AND QUESTIONS:

¹³ Someone in the crowd said to him, "Teacher, tell my brother to divide the inheritance with me."

¹⁴ Jesus replied, "Man, who appointed me a judge or an arbiter between you?" ¹⁵ Then he said to them, "Watch out! Be on your guard against all kinds of greed; a man's life does not consist in the abundance of his possessions."

¹⁶ And he told them this parable: "The ground of a certain rich man produced a good crop. ¹⁷ He thought to himself, 'What shall I do? I have no place to store my crops.'

¹⁸ "Then he said, 'This is what I'll do. I will tear down my barns and build bigger ones, and there I will store all my grain and my goods. ¹⁹ And I'll say to myself, "You have plenty of good things laid up for many years. Take life easy; eat, drink and be merry."'

²⁰ "But God said to him, 'You fool! This very night your life will be demanded from you. Then who will get what you have prepared for yourself?'

²¹ "This is how it will be with anyone who stores up things for himself but is not rich toward God."

*1. What does the demand in verse 13 reveal about the man making it?*

*2. Why does Jesus associate the man's question with greed? What is greed?*

*3. What was wrong with the rich fool's reasoning? What did he assume to be in his control that was not?*

## Day Two Reading and Questions:

22 Then Jesus said to his disciples: "Therefore I tell you, do not worry about your life, what you will eat; or about your body, what you will wear. 23 Life is more than food, and the body more than clothes. 24 Consider the ravens: They do not sow or reap, they have no storeroom or barn; yet God feeds them. And how much more valuable you are than birds! 25 Who of you by worrying can add a single hour to his life? 26 Since you cannot do this very little thing, why do you worry about the rest?

27 "Consider how the lilies grow. They do not labor or spin. Yet I tell you, not even Solomon in all his splendor was dressed like one of these. 28 If that is how God clothes the grass of the field, which is here today, and tomorrow is thrown into the fire, how much more will he clothe you, O you of little faith! 29 And do not set your heart on what you will eat or drink; do not worry about it. 30 For the pagan world runs after all such things, and your Father knows that you need them. 31 But seek his kingdom, and these things will be given to you as well.

32 "Do not be afraid, little flock, for your Father has been pleased to give you the kingdom. 33 Sell your possessions and give to the poor. Provide purses for yourselves that will not wear out, a treasure in heaven that will not be exhausted, where no thief comes near and no moth destroys. 34 For where your treasure is, there your heart will be also.

*1. Do you think it is possible not to worry about **anything**? Why or why not?*

*2. What causes us to worry? What is the solution to worry?*

*3. What is "the kingdom" that is promised and what relationship does it have to fear?*

## DAY THREE READING AND QUESTIONS:

[35] "Be dressed ready for service and keep your lamps burning, [36] like men waiting for their master to return from a wedding banquet, so that when he comes and knocks they can immediately open the door for him. [37] It will be good for those servants whose master finds them watching when he comes. I tell you the truth, he will dress himself to serve, will have them recline at the table and will come and wait on them. [38] It will be good for those servants whose master finds them ready, even if he comes in the second or third watch of the night. [39] But understand this: If the owner of the house had known at what hour the thief was coming, he would not have let his house be broken into. [40] You also must be ready, because the Son of Man will come at an hour when you do not expect him."

[41] Peter asked, "Lord, are you telling this parable to us, or to everyone?"

[42] The Lord answered, "Who then is the faithful and wise manager, whom the master puts in charge of his servants to give them their food allowance at the proper time? [43] It will be good for that servant whom the master finds doing so when he returns. [44] I tell you the truth, he will put him in charge of all his possessions. [45] But suppose the servant says to himself, 'My master is taking a long time in coming,' and he then begins to beat the menservants and maidservants and to eat and drink and get drunk. [46] The master of that servant will come on a day when he does not expect him and at an hour he is not aware of. He will cut him to pieces and assign him a place with the unbelievers.

[47] "That servant who knows his master's will and does not get ready or does not do what his master wants will be beaten with many blows. [48] But the one who does not know and does things deserving punishment will be beaten with few blows. From everyone who has been given much, much will be demanded; and from the one who has been entrusted with much, much more will be asked.

*1. How do we keep dressed for action with our lamps lit?*

*2. Was does Peter's question reveal?*

*3. Why is it important to know that more will be expected from one who is entrusted with much?*

## Day Four Reading and Questions:

[49] "I have come to bring fire on the earth, and how I wish it were already kindled! [50] But I have a baptism to undergo, and how distressed I am until it is completed! [51] Do you think I came to bring peace on earth? No, I tell you, but division. [52] From now on there will be five in one family divided against each other, three against two and two against three. [53] They will be divided, father against son and son against father, mother against daughter and daughter against mother, mother-in-law against daughter-in-law and daughter-in-law against mother-in-law."

[54] He said to the crowd: "When you see a cloud rising in the west, immediately you say, 'It's going to rain,' and it does. [55] And when the south wind blows, you say, 'It's going to be hot,' and it is. [56] Hypocrites! You know how to interpret the appearance of the earth and the sky. How is it that you don't know how to interpret this present time?

[57] "Why don't you judge for yourselves what is right? [58] As you are going with your adversary to the magistrate, try hard to be reconciled to him on the way, or he may drag you off to the judge, and the judge turn you over to the officer, and the officer throw you into prison. [59] I tell you, you will not get out until you have paid the last penny.'"

*1. If Jesus is the Prince of Peace, why does he here speak of division?*

*2. Why is the kingdom message divisive?*

*3. What does the ability to predict the weather have to do with the kingdom of God?*

## Day Five Reading and Questions:

Reread the entire passage (12:13-59).

*1. How does greed affect your life? Do you regard what you have as a reflection of who you are?*

*2. Is it possible to participate in the kingdom to such an extent that we have no concerns in this world? If so, how do we learn to experience such a life?*

*3. Are you living in anticipation of the Lord's return? Why or why not?*

# MEDITATION

Good news, bad news again, right? There is much to rejoice about in these readings, along with very troubling teachings. If we choose to live in submission to the will of God, all is well. But life outside his kingdom is a scary place to be. How much sense does it make to live for things that have no real meaning or value? Who told us it was meaningful to amass wealth we cannot use while others starve? Are we living the life of the rich fool? Jesus has a solution to living for wealth—live in God's kingdom! Life is more than food, and the body more than clothes! God calls us to a more meaningful life. Does he not show us through nature that he will care for us? Now, it makes sense for the person who does not believe in a loving, caring God to worry. But for one who lives in God's care? It is nonsense to worry. I once saw a church marquee that read, "Why pray when you can worry?" Point well taken. How can we pray and still worry? Simply because we choose to live in the wrong world. Where God is in control, there is no place for worry or fear.

We need to live in anticipation of his coming. The last two readings call us to live in participation in his work, so that when he comes we will be ready. We will be held responsible for what we have been given. And we know that he will come again. Here's the question, "Are we living in such a way that we would have no regrets if he came in this moment?" That is a hard question to answer, but it is also a great motivator for not throwing our lives away in the pursuit of meaningless things.

Rather than seeing this as a doomsday warning, we should see this as a serious call to life in God's kingdom. It is not easy. The kingdom of God is not a subject about which people can be neutral. It divides families. Why? Because kingdom life is not compatible with worldly life. Too many of use try to live in both worlds. Instead of

LUKE: JESUS IS SAVIOR

calling people out of the world and into the kingdom, we have settled for making friends with the world. That is a dangerous place to be.

We who believe, know the Lord will return. We do not know when. But we do know what will happen when he comes. All will be called to give an account of their lives. Are we wise enough to live in God's future now?

"God of wisdom and glory, free me from my desire to amass worthless things and instead guide me to pursue your purposes for my life. Help me live in joyful anticipation of your return."

# A NEW PERSPECTIVE FOR LIFE
## (Luke 13:1-21)

### Day One Reading and Questions:

[1] Now there were some present at that time who told Jesus about the Galileans whose blood Pilate had mixed with their sacrifices. [2] Jesus answered, "Do you think that these Galileans were worse sinners than all the other Galileans because they suffered this way? [3] I tell you, no! But unless you repent, you too will all perish. [4] Or those eighteen who died when the tower in Siloam fell on them—do you think they were more guilty than all the others living in Jerusalem? [5] I tell you, no! But unless you repent, you too will all perish."

1. How did Jesus respond to the question about the cause of seemingly unlucky or unmerited deaths?

2. What does "repentance" have to do with this? Do all of us really need to repent?

3. In what sense will we perish if we do not repent?

### Day Two Reading and Questions:

[6] Then he told this parable: "A man had a fig tree, planted in his vineyard, and he went to look for fruit on it, but did not find any. [7] So

he said to the man who took care of the vineyard, 'For three years now I've been coming to look for fruit on this fig tree and haven't found any. Cut it down! Why should it use up the soil?'

⁸ " 'Sir,' the man replied, 'leave it alone for one more year, and I'll dig around it and fertilize it. ⁹ If it bears fruit next year, fine! If not, then cut it down.' "

*1. What was the purpose of planting the fig tree? How does this apply to us?*

*2. Why did the owner want the fig tree cut down?*

*3. Why did the gardener ask to give the tree another chance? How did the owner respond?*

## Day Three Reading and Questions:

¹⁰ On a Sabbath Jesus was teaching in one of the synagogues, ¹¹ and a woman was there who had been crippled by a spirit for eighteen years. She was bent over and could not straighten up at all. ¹² When Jesus saw her, he called her forward and said to her, "Woman, you are set free from your infirmity." ¹³ Then he put his hands on her, and immediately she straightened up and praised God.

¹⁴ Indignant because Jesus had healed on the Sabbath, the synagogue ruler said to the people, "There are six days for work. So come and be healed on those days, not on the Sabbath."

¹⁵ The Lord answered him, "You hypocrites! Doesn't each of you on the Sabbath untie his ox or donkey from the stall and lead it out to give it water? ¹⁶ Then should not this woman, a daughter of Abraham, whom Satan has kept bound for eighteen long years, be set free on the Sabbath day from what bound her?"

<sup>17</sup> When he said this, all his opponents were humiliated, but the people were delighted with all the wonderful things he was doing.

*1. Why is it significant that the lady had been crippled for so long?*

*2. What did the women do when healed and why?*

*3. What does the response of the leader of the synagogue tell us about his heart?*

## DAY FOUR READING AND QUESTIONS:

<sup>18</sup> Then Jesus asked, "What is the kingdom of God like? What shall I compare it to? <sup>19</sup> It is like a mustard seed, which a man took and planted in his garden. It grew and became a tree, and the birds of the air perched in its branches."

<sup>20</sup> Again he asked, "What shall I compare the kingdom of God to? <sup>21</sup> It is like yeast that a woman took and mixed into a large amount of flour until it worked all through the dough."

*1. How is the kingdom of God like a mustard seed? What do you think Jesus was teaching with this illustration?*

*2. How is the kingdom of God like yeast?*

*3. What should these two illustrations mean to us?*

## DAY FIVE READING AND QUESTIONS:

Reread the entire passage (13:1-21).

*1. Of what, do you think, would Jesus call us to repent?*

2. *What does the parable of the fig tree call us to consider about our own lives?*

3. *Are there times we've allowed our concern for law to trump our desire to help someone in need? What can we do to make sure our regard for God's law truly honors him?*

# MEDITATION

Hardly a day goes by without tragedies in our world reminding us that life is fragile. Not long ago a strong wind weakened a tree's roots. Without warning, long after the storm, the tree fell and crushed a passing car. The driver lost his life. So life has been from the beginning. How do we make sense of such things? Or, how do we account for evil individuals who cause the death of other human beings with seeming disregard for life? Jesus' answer is one we likely do not want to hear—unless we repent, we too will perish. So, is sin the cause of accidental deaths? Jesus is not attempting to explain why these things happen; he is reminding us there is only one place to live with security—and that is in the kingdom of God. There we have no need for fear, even of death, if we are living a life that will not end. Life is fragile! Jesus invites us to repent from our self-centered lives and live where God controls our eternal destiny. Otherwise, we will perish.

We are slow to hear the consistent teachings of Jesus about the purpose of our lives. There is only one—to bear fruit for God in the kingdom. If we are not living for God's purposes and bearing the fruit of his love and character, we need to realize we are living on borrowed time. This parable calls us to evaluate our lives—what are we producing in our lives that brings glory to God? If we are living only for ourselves, the call from Jesus is unambiguous, "Repent."

The story of the crippled woman is another heart breaker. Rather than rejoicing with a woman who stood up for the first time in eighteen years, the religious leaders were offended at Jesus' perceived violation of a religious rule. Once again, Jesus called them to task—how could they be so "two-faced"? Acting as if they cared about God's purposes, all they really cared about was themselves. They could assist their own distressed farm animals on the Sabbath, but would not allow Jesus to free a fellow child of Abraham from her infirmity. We have seen enough of these examples to ask ourselves the question, "Have I created a religious system that is convenient for my own self-centered purposes, or am I truly attempting to be God's servant?"

For the nature of the kingdom is such that if we will just do a little, God can make that offering grow into much. With the example of the mustard seed and super yeast, we are reminded that God is the one who causes the growth, and he is amazing in his power! So once again we are called to live in the kingdom, where there is no fear of death, where God constantly provides opportunities to do good, and where little becomes much because God is at work through us!

"Almighty Creator, I cannot fathom why you have invited me to live under your loving guidance. Help me to learn to live more fully submitted to you every day. May my actions be like the mustard seed and yeast, all to your glory."

# THE NARROW DOOR AND HARD HEARTS

## (Luke 13:22-14:6)

### DAY ONE READING AND QUESTIONS:

²² Then Jesus went through the towns and villages, teaching as he made his way to Jerusalem. ²³ Someone asked him, "Lord, are only a few people going to be saved?"

He said to them, ²⁴ "Make every effort to enter through the narrow door, because many, I tell you, will try to enter and will not be able to. ²⁵ Once the owner of the house gets up and closes the door, you will stand outside knocking and pleading, 'Sir, open the door for us.'

"But he will answer, 'I don't know you or where you come from.'

²⁶ "Then you will say, 'We ate and drank with you, and you taught in our streets.'

²⁷ "But he will reply, 'I don't know you or where you come from. Away from me, all you evildoers!'

²⁸ "There will be weeping there, and gnashing of teeth, when you see Abraham, Isaac and Jacob and all the prophets in the kingdom of God, but you yourselves thrown out.

*1. Why did the disciples ask Jesus if only a few would be saved?*

*2. What is the meaning of Jesus' response, in your thinking?*

*3. Is it possible for us to believe we follow Jesus when in reality we don't? How could this happen?*

## DAY TWO READING AND QUESTIONS:

²⁹ People will come from east and west and north and south, and
will take their places at the feast in the kingdom of God. ³⁰ Indeed
there are those who are last who will be first, and first who will be last."
³¹ At that time some Pharisees came to Jesus and said to him, "Leave
this place and go somewhere else. Herod wants to kill you."

³² He replied, "Go tell that fox, 'I will drive out demons and heal
people today and tomorrow, and on the third day I will reach my
goal.' ³³ In any case, I must keep going today and tomorrow and the
next day—for surely no prophet can die outside Jerusalem!

> 1. *What is the meaning of people coming from every direction to eat in*
>    *the kingdom of God while those who thought they knew God would*
>    *not be allowed in?*
>
> 2. *How does the "last being first and first last" fit in this passage?*
>
> 3. *Do you think the Pharisees were actually concerned with Jesus'*
>    *well being?*

## DAY THREE READING AND QUESTIONS:

³⁴ O Jerusalem, Jerusalem, you who kill the prophets and stone
those sent to you, how often I have longed to gather your children
together, as a hen gathers her chicks under her wings, but you were
not willing! ³⁵ Look, your house is left to you desolate. I tell you, you
will not see me again until you say, 'Blessed is he who comes in the
name of the Lord.'"

1. Why did Jesus cry over Jerusalem?

2. How had Jerusalem repeatedly refused God's call to submission to
His will?

3. How is it that the city would not "see" Jesus until he comes in the
name of the Lord?

## DAY FOUR READING AND QUESTIONS:

14:1 One Sabbath, when Jesus went to eat in the house of a promi-
nent Pharisee, he was being carefully watched. 2 There in front of him
was a man suffering from dropsy. 3 Jesus asked the Pharisees and
experts in the law, "Is it lawful to heal on the Sabbath or not?" 4 But
they remained silent. So taking hold of the man, he healed him and
sent him away.

5 Then he asked them, "If one of you has a son or an ox that falls
into a well on the Sabbath day, will you not immediately pull him
out?" 6 And they had nothing to say.

1. Why were the Pharisees watching Jesus so closely? What did they fail
to see?

2. Why were the Pharisees and experts in the Law quiet when Jesus
asked them about the legality of healing on the Sabbath?

3. Why do you think this issue keeps coming up?

### Day Five Reading and Questions:

Reread the entire passage (13:22-14:6).

> 1. *Jesus instructs us to make every effort to enter through the narrow door. What efforts can we make to do this?*

> 2. *What does Jesus' answer to Herod demonstrate about his faith in God? What can we learn from this?*

> 3. *Do you think Jesus would weep over our cities today as he did over Jerusalem? Why or why not?*

## MEDITATION

Something in Jesus' teaching unsettled his listeners. As the time of his death drew nearer, his teachings were more pointed, calling for repentance from all. It led someone to ask if only a few would be saved. Jesus did not answer the question—rather, he spoke of how many would not be saved. His response calls us all to immediate action. We must all make every effort to enter the narrow door while it is open. The door is narrow because the life of true discipleship is difficult. But the consequences of not entering are much more severe. Others will come and take our places if we choose not to enter while the door is open.

Jesus' constant challenge to the Jews is one we must hear. He warned them of a day that God would say, "I do not know you." How could this be? They would argue of their relationship with God, of hearing his word, and eating at his table. But in truth, they did not know God. It is one thing to know about God, another to know God.

Day Four's reading brings up another event that demonstrates how far the religious leaders were from God. It is another Sabbath debacle—Jesus asked if he should heal on the Sabbath and they remained silent. Had they really known God, they would have quickly responded, "Yes, particularly on the Sabbath, because the Sabbath is about knowing and trusting God." But they had nothing to say.

Jesus lived in a world apart from the religious leaders that surrounded him. Were they genuinely concerned when they warned Jesus of Herod's threats? We cannot say for sure. But this we know—Jesus was not the least bit troubled by Herod. Why? Because he did not live in Herod's world. He lived in a world where his Father was in control. And he knew God's purposes for him could not be thwarted if he remained faithful. Because he lived in God's world, when he looked at Jerusalem he did not see impressive buildings and bustling trade. He saw what it would one day be because of its unbelief.

So here is the question, once again. Where do you live? What do you fear? What are you earnestly striving to do? How do you see hurting people in need of help? Here is the challenge—make every effort to enter the narrow door of discipleship into the world where God will direct your life. It is a dramatically different place than that where most choose to live.

"Faithful Lord, show me the way into your kingdom. Give me the courage to enter the narrow door that I may dwell in the presence of God and hear his voice."

# TABLE BEHAVIOR AND A DINNER INVITATION

## (Luke 14:7-24)

### DAY ONE READING AND QUESTIONS:

[7] When he noticed how the guests picked the places of honor at the table, he told them this parable: [8] "When someone invites you to a wedding feast, do not take the place of honor, for a person more distinguished than you may have been invited. [9] If so, the host who invited both of you will come and say to you, 'Give this man your seat.' Then, humiliated, you will have to take the least important place. [10] But when you are invited, take the lowest place, so that when your host comes, he will say to you, 'Friend, move up to a better place.' Then you will be honored in the presence of all your fellow guests. [11] For everyone who exalts himself will be humbled, and he who humbles himself will be exalted."

*1. What did Jesus notice that caused Him to tell a parable?*

*2. Why do you think Jesus called to task the idea of "table status"?*

*3. Do you think Jesus was really trying to give the people a strategy for getting more attention?*

## Day Two Reading and Questions:

¹² Then Jesus said to his host, "When you give a luncheon or dinner, do not invite your friends, your brothers or relatives, or your rich neighbors; if you do, they may invite you back and so you will be repaid. ¹³ But when you give a banquet, invite the poor, the crippled, the lame, the blind, ¹⁴ and you will be blessed. Although they cannot repay you, you will be repaid at the resurrection of the righteous."

*1. Was Jesus saying it is wrong to invite friends and relatives over for a meal?*

*2. If not, what is Jesus teaching us with these words?*

*3. Why should we invite those to our tables who have nothing to give?*

## Day Three Reading and Questions:

¹⁵ When one of those at the table with him heard this, he said to Jesus, "Blessed is the man who will eat at the feast in the kingdom of God."

¹⁶ Jesus replied: "A certain man was preparing a great banquet and invited many guests. ¹⁷ At the time of the banquet he sent his servant to tell those who had been invited, 'Come, for everything is now ready.'

¹⁸ "But they all alike began to make excuses. The first said, 'I have just bought a field, and I must go and see it. Please excuse me.'

¹⁹ "Another said, 'I have just bought five yoke of oxen, and I'm on my way to try them out. Please excuse me.'

²⁰ "Still another said, 'I just got married, so I can't come.'

*1. What do you think the one who shouted out a blessing was trying to say? (v. 15)*

*2. What was the great dinner Jesus referred to in this parable?*

*3. Do you consider these excuses valid? Why or why not?*

## DAY FOUR READING AND QUESTIONS:

[21] "The servant came back and reported this to his master. Then the owner of the house became angry and ordered his servant, 'Go out quickly into the streets and alleys of the town and bring in the poor, the crippled, the blind and the lame.'

[22] " 'Sir,' the servant said, 'what you ordered has been done, but there is still room.'

[23] "Then the master told his servant, 'Go out to the roads and country lanes and make them come in, so that my house will be full. [24] I tell you, not one of those men who were invited will get a taste of my banquet.' "

*1. What did the slave report to his master?*

*2. What was the master's reaction?*

*3. What was Jesus teaching us with this parable?*

## DAY FIVE READING AND QUESTIONS:

Reread the entire passage (14:7-24).

*1. How do we claim status in today's world? How do you think Jesus would react to this?*

2. *Host a "kingdom meal." Intentionally invite guests to a fine meal who cannot reciprocate. Invite a homeless person, a minimum wage earner, someone unemployed—see what God does.*

3. *What is the basic difference between those originally invited and those who finally came to the great banquet? What does this tell us of the danger of living a life of plenty?*

## MEDITATION

One of the great lessons we can learn from Jesus is how to recognize teachable moments. He often found himself in situations that provided a wonderful example, allowing him to expound on the true nature of God's kingdom. The table was a central fixture in the culture of Jesus' day. It was not only where one ate, but also where one claimed his proper status. There are still cultures in our world that practice "status seating." It is a fascinating thing to watch. The host takes his or her place at the head of the table. The honored guest is seated at the right hand of the host, the second most important at the left—and so on. People coming to the table look around nervously, to make sure they are properly assessing where they should sit. It was this dynamic that Jesus noticed. Was he bemused or angered by it? I believe he simply wanted to show how meaningless the whole idea really is. His strategy was not to be taken seriously. Can you imagine Jesus teaching us how to manipulate a situation to receive higher glory? He was poking fun—but his concluding point was certainly true: "Everyone who exalts himself will be humbled, and he who humbles himself will be exalted."

Jesus then issues a startling challenge, one few have heard to this day. We live in a world of reciprocity. By nature, we invite those to our table who will return the favor. We invite friends, family, or rich neighbors. While there is nothing wrong with this, it is not kingdom living. If we choose to live where God is in control of our lives, we will invite those who cannot pay us back. And this type of hospitality can be shown far beyond the meal itself. Whom do we choose to befriend at work or at school? What criteria do we use to decide who plays on our team or rides in our carpool? What a challenge! Trust Jesus. Free yourself from the world of quid pro quo (I'll do this for you if you'll do this for me) and find life!

What can we learn from the parable of the great banquet? There is no valid excuse for turning down the invitation of God to dine at his table. Jesus here implied that the Jews were missing their greatest opportunity. They had been invited into the kingdom, but they were so busy with life as they knew it, they refused the invitation to come. We must not miss God's invitation to dine with him on a daily basis in his kingdom. What is our excuse? Why do we choose to live in the world of our own making rather than under God's reign?

"Lord of the banquet table, open my eyes to those I should invite into my life. Free me from the need of the approval of the 'successful' or 'wealthy.' As I dine daily at the banquet table of your kingdom, give me a heart of compassion for the poor, the crippled, the lame, and the blind."

# THE COST OF DISCIPLESHIP

## (Luke 14:25-34)

### Day One Reading and Questions:

<sup>25</sup> Large crowds were traveling with Jesus, and turning to them he said: <sup>26</sup> "If anyone comes to me and does not hate his father and mother, his wife and children, his brothers and sisters-yes, even his own life-he cannot be my disciple. <sup>27</sup> And anyone who does not carry his cross and follow me cannot be my disciple.

*1. Why do you think Jesus chose this particular time to present such a difficult teaching?*

*2. What do you think Jesus meant by "hate" in this context?*

*3. What is the cross we are called to carry?*

### Day Two Reading and Questions:

<sup>28</sup> "Suppose one of you wants to build a tower. Will he not first sit down and estimate the cost to see if he has enough money to complete it? <sup>29</sup> For if he lays the foundation and is not able to finish it, everyone who sees it will ridicule him, <sup>30</sup> saying, 'This fellow began to build and was not able to finish.'

*1. Why do you think Jesus used the example of building a tower?*

*2. What would cause the tower builder ultimate embarrassment?*

*3. What application does this have to discipleship?*

## Day Three Reading and Questions:

[31] "Or suppose a king is about to go to war against another king. Will he not first sit down and consider whether he is able with ten thousand men to oppose the one coming against him with twenty thousand? [32] If he is not able, he will send a delegation while the other is still a long way off and will ask for terms of peace. [33] In the same way, any of you who does not give up everything he has cannot be my disciple.

*1. What does the example of a king waging war add to Jesus' teaching about commitment in discipleship?*

*2. What might Jesus be saying about discipleship when he suggests it is similar to a king who would be better off conceding defeat and seeking peace?*

*3. Do you believe Jesus actually meant we must give up all our possessions in order to be a disciple?*

## Day Four Reading and Questions:

[34] "Salt is good, but if it loses its saltiness, how can it be made salty again? [35] It is fit neither for the soil nor for the manure pile; it is thrown out.

"He who has ears to hear, let him hear."

*1. How does salt lose its taste?*

*2. What does this have to do with Jesus' teaching on discipleship?*

*3. What does Jesus want us to hear in these verses?*

### Day Five Reading and Questions:

Reread the entire passage (14:25-34).

*1. What is the proper relationship between our families, Jesus, and us?*

*2. How does one "hate" his own life? What do you think Jesus meant by this?*

*3. What is the cost of discipleship for you personally?*

## MEDITATION

How are we to understand Jesus' teaching that one of the conditions of discipleship is to hate those dearest to us? Should one actually hate oneself? Is that healthy?

It is important to understand what Jesus is saying as well as what he is not saying. In the last reading, Jesus told a parable about some who refused to come to the table of God because they had a higher allegiance to people or things. Clearly, we must never allow anyone or anything to get in the way of our relationship to God. Repeatedly, Jesus has made it clear that the only way to truly follow him is with undivided loyalty. Jesus demonstrates this relationship in his obedience to his father. We must have the same relationship with him. If we do not love him more than all, we do not love him at all.

Jesus' instruction to "hate" is a form of exaggeration common in his day. It is a manner of comparison: our love for Jesus must be of such magnitude that our love for other people or things looks like hate in comparison. This is not about loving others less; it is about loving Jesus more. It is only in this kind of loyalty to and love for Jesus that we can find true life, even if such devotion leads to physical death. This is the cross he calls us to bear daily. To his glory, we bear the sign of death, in order to find life.

One of today's biggest challenges to authentic discipleship is divided loyalty. Perhaps more accurately, in our culture, we struggle with a splintered loyalty. There are so many things competing for our time and hearts. We find ourselves trying to balance work, family, recreation, social needs, and church responsibilities. No wonder we lack focus! Jesus came to show us a way out of the frantic pace many of us battle. Love him beyond all else, and we will find life.

Jesus gives us one more illustration of authentic discipleship—salt. It was a valuable substance in Jesus' day, even more so than in ours. It was traded as currency in some cultures. It had many uses. If mixed with enough dirt, however, it lost all value. Discipleship is like salt—if it is pure, it is of great value. It can be used for many things. A diluted discipleship has no value to anyone.

Have you counted the cost? There is great promise to the world around you when you declare your intent to walk as an apprentice with Jesus. The road is not easy. It calls for your full commitment. There is no "part time" option.

"Dear Lord, help me give my life fully to you. Keep me focused on your purposes. May I be like pure salt to those around me that they may know you."

# REJOICE THE LOST IS FOUND!
## (Luke 15)

### Day One Reading and Questions:

¹ Now the tax collectors and "sinners" were all gathering around to hear him. ² But the Pharisees and the teachers of the law muttered, "This man welcomes sinners and eats with them."

*1. Why do you think the sinners and tax collectors were coming near and listening to Jesus?*

*2. Why did this so upset the Pharisees and the teachers of the law?*

*3. Are we attractive to the sinners and outcasts of our culture? Why or why not?*

### Day Two Reading and Questions:

³ Then Jesus told them this parable: ⁴ "Suppose one of you has a hundred sheep and loses one of them. Does he not leave the ninety-nine in the open country and go after the lost sheep until he finds it? ⁵ And when he finds it, he joyfully puts it on his shoulders ⁶ and goes home. Then he calls his friends and neighbors together and says, 'Rejoice with me; I have found my lost sheep.' ⁷ I tell you that in the same way there will be more rejoicing in heaven over one sinner who repents than over ninety-nine righteous persons who do not need to repent.

*1. Why is the one lost sheep so inordinately important?*

*2. What caused the rejoicing?*

*3. What do you think Jesus wanted those hearing this parable to under-stand about God?*

## Day Three Reading and Questions:

[8] "Or suppose a woman has ten silver coins and loses one. Does she not light a lamp, sweep the house and search carefully until she finds it? [9] And when she finds it, she calls her friends and neighbors together and says, 'Rejoice with me; I have found my lost coin.' [10] In the same way, I tell you, there is rejoicing in the presence of the angels of God over one sinner who repents."

*1. Why did this woman spend so much time looking for a lost coin? Why wouldn't she settle for having nine?*

*2. If the woman was worried about losing the one coin because of its value, why would she then spend money on a party to celebrate its being found?*

*3. According to this story, what makes the angels of heaven rejoice?*

## Day Four Reading and Questions:

[11] Jesus continued: "There was a man who had two sons. [12] The younger one said to his father, 'Father, give me my share of the estate.' So he divided his property between them.

[13] "Not long after that, the younger son got together all he had, set off for a distant country and there squandered his wealth in wild living. [14] After he had spent everything, there was a severe famine in that whole country, and he began to be in need. [15] So he went and hired himself out to a citizen of that country, who sent him to his fields to feed pigs. [16] He longed to fill his stomach with the pods that the pigs were eating, but no one gave him anything.

[17] "When he came to his senses, he said, 'How many of my father's hired men have food to spare, and here I am starving to death! [18] I will set out and go back to my father and say to him: Father, I have sinned against heaven and against you. [19] I am no longer worthy to be called your son; make me like one of your hired men.' [20] So he got up and went to his father.

"But while he was still a long way off, his father saw him and was filled with compassion for him; he ran to his son, threw his arms around him and kissed him.

[21] "The son said to him, 'Father, I have sinned against heaven and against you. I am no longer worthy to be called your son.'

[22] "But the father said to his servants, 'Quick! Bring the best robe and put it on him. Put a ring on his finger and sandals on his feet. [23] Bring the fattened calf and kill it. Let's have a feast and celebrate. [24] For this son of mine was dead and is alive again; he was lost and is found.' So they began to celebrate.

[25] "Meanwhile, the older son was in the field. When he came near the house, he heard music and dancing. [26] So he called one of the servants and asked him what was going on. [27] 'Your brother has come,' he replied, 'and your father has killed the fattened calf because he has him back safe and sound.'

[28] "The older brother became angry and refused to go in. So his father went out and pleaded with him. [29] But he answered his father, 'Look! All these years I've been slaving for you and never disobeyed your orders. Yet you never gave me even a young goat so I could

celebrate with my friends. ³⁰ But when this son of yours who has squandered your property with prostitutes comes home, you kill the fattened calf for him!'

³¹ " 'My son,' the father said, 'you are always with me, and everything I have is yours. ³² But we had to celebrate and be glad, because this brother of yours was dead and is alive again; he was lost and is found.' "

1. *What caused the young man eventually to want to return home? What role did he seek?*

2. *Why did the older brother object to the celebration of the younger's return?*

3. *Which of the brothers suffered the most from their wrongful attitude and why?*

## Day Five Reading and Questions:

Reread the entire passage (15:1-32).

1. *Have you ever been totally lost? Recall the emotions of the experience. Recall the joy of being found or finding your way.*

2. *Have you ever lost something of great value and then found it? Do you remember the joy of finding it? Describe that joy.*

3. *Describe the love of the father for both sons, and then reflect on God's love for you.*

# MEDITATION

Celebration is the natural response when the lost is found. The greater the value of the object, the greater the celebration. Why, then, did the religious leaders around Jesus not celebrate when sinners (the lost) came to him seeking help? That's the purpose of these three stories. The problem they confront is not the lost, but those who have no concern for the lost.

The reading begins with the disgust expressed by the Pharisees and teachers of the law because Jesus was eating with sinners. The irony here is thick—the table from which they wanted to exclude sinners was the feast from which they barred themselves by their self-righteous attitudes.

Is it possible we at times do the same thing? When we use the table of God to exclude the world from his presence instead of inviting them to his feast, it is time to repent! When we use the Lord's Table as a sign of our righteousness instead of a celebration of God's gracious provision for all, we must repent! We gather at God's table to celebrate his wondrous love and forgiveness. As we look around, we see that there are not enough people at the table! The abundance of wonderful food could feed the entire world if they would come! The Lord's Table should compel us to go out to the highways and byways and invite the poor, suffering, and those neglected by the world to the table of plenty!

Whether one of a hundred, or one of ten, or one of two, if it is lost, God is seeking it. Whether it be out of mindless wandering (the sheep), no fault of its own (the coin), or intentional disobedience (the son), God's loving grace seeks to bring the lost home. And when the lost is found, there is great rejoicing! This is a great demonstration of God's heart! Do we have his heart in us?

Of these stories, we identify most easily with that of the prodigal son. The foolish young son shows disdain for his father's possessions. He chafes to break free from his "oppression." He wants what is "his" to spend as he desires. Surprisingly, the father concedes. It does not take long for the son to realize his folly. He quickly spends his wealth and his desperate circumstances bring him to realize the servants of his father are far better off that he is. Deeply repentant and knowing he deserves severe punishment, he starts his long walk home. Have you wondered why Jesus tells us so much about the prodigal if the story is to discipline the elder brother? Because we, who tend to be that older brother, need to be aware of the process of repentance that brings sinners home! The father knew his prodigal son's heart! He knew what he had been through. That's why punishment was not appropriate. The son's heart had been broken; he knew of his sin— what he needed was a way home.

The father's response is one we can never forget. He puts a robe on his son, gives him the signet ring (full access to the wealth of the estate), and calls for an immediate feast! Here comes the point of the story. When the older brother hears what has happened, he is indignant. Why hadn't the father thrown him a party? Where was his reward for his faithful labor all these years? He had completely missed the feast of relationship he could have had with his father. He had reduced it to duty. In truth, his heart was no closer to the father's than his brother's was when he was in the far country.

Who are we in this story? Are we the repentant son? If so, celebrate the wonder of the grace of God! Are we the older brother? Repent and rejoice with the lost when they turn back to God. I think Jesus is calling us to be the father—to be the ones looking down the road for the broken who are looking for a way to come home. So, let's stock up on the robes, have the rings at hand, be ready to throw a party. Forgive extravagantly, and join in the heavenly celebration of the lost being found!

"Forgiving Father, teach us to join you in looking down the road, with hearts longing for sinners to come home. Give us eyes to see repentant hearts, give us wisdom to respond as you respond, and give us the heart to embrace them as you would."

# PRIZED BY HUMANS, DETESTED BY GOD

### (Luke 16:1-18)

## DAY ONE READING AND QUESTIONS

[1] Jesus told his disciples: "There was a rich man whose manager was accused of wasting his possessions. [2] So he called him in and asked him, 'What is this I hear about you? Give an account of your management, because you cannot be manager any longer.'

[3] "The manager said to himself, 'What shall I do now? My master is taking away my job. I'm not strong enough to dig, and I'm ashamed to beg— [4] I know what I'll do so that, when I lose my job here, people will welcome me into their houses.'

[5] "So he called in each one of his master's debtors. He asked the first, 'How much do you owe my master?'

[6] " 'Eight hundred gallons of olive oil,' he replied.

"The manager told him, 'Take your bill, sit down quickly, and make it four hundred.'

[7] "Then he asked the second, 'And how much do you owe?'

" 'A thousand bushels of wheat,' he replied.

"He told him, 'Take your bill and make it eight hundred.'

[8] "The master commended the dishonest manager because he had acted shrewdly. For the people of this world are more shrewd in dealing with their own kind than are the people of the light. [9] I tell you, use worldly wealth to gain friends for yourselves, so that when it is gone, you will be welcomed into eternal dwellings.

*1. Do you think the manager was indeed squandering the rich man's property?*

*2. What was the greatest fear of the manager?*

*3. What are the good qualities of the manager?*

## DAY TWO READING AND QUESTIONS:

[10] "Whoever can be trusted with very little can also be trusted with much, and whoever is dishonest with very little will also be dishonest with much. [11] So if you have not been trustworthy in handling worldly wealth, who will trust you with true riches? [12] And if you have not been trustworthy with someone else's property, who will give you property of your own?

[13] "No servant can serve two masters. Either he will hate the one and love the other, or he will be devoted to the one and despise the other. You cannot serve both God and Money."

*1. How can we be faithful with wealth?*

*2. What are the "true riches" with which we might be entrusted?*

*3. Why can't we serve God and wealth?*

## DAY THREE READING AND QUESTIONS:

[14] The Pharisees, who loved money, heard all this and were sneering at Jesus. [15] He said to them, "You are the ones who justify

yourselves in the eyes of men, but God knows your hearts. What is highly valued among men is detestable in God's sight.

1. *Why do you think the Pharisees ridiculed Jesus for his teaching?*

2. *What do you think Jesus was referring to when he accused the Pharisees of justifying themselves?*

3. *To what is Jesus referring when he says there are things prized by man that are abominations to God?*

## DAY FOUR READING AND QUESTIONS:

[16] "The Law and the Prophets were proclaimed until John. Since that time, the good news of the kingdom of God is being preached, and everyone is forcing his way into it. [17] It is easier for heaven and earth to disappear than for the least stroke of a pen to drop out of the Law.

[18] "Anyone who divorces his wife and marries another woman commits adultery, and the man who marries a divorced woman commits adultery.

1. *What do you think Jesus means when he says everyone attempts to enter the kingdom of God by force?*

2. *What does this have to do with every point of the law standing?*

3. *Why do you think Jesus mentions divorce and remarriage in this context?*

## DAY FIVE READING AND QUESTIONS:

Reread the entire passage (16:1-18).

1. *What does Jesus instruct us to do with wealth? What do you think he means by this?*

2. *Do you really believe it is impossible to serve God and wealth? Why or why not?*

3. *What do you think is Jesus' main point in this reading? How will that point affect your life?*

# MEDITATION

The parable of the shrewd manager is difficult to understand. Is Jesus really teaching us to be dishonest at worst or shrewd at best in order to make money that will have eternal benefit? Or might he be telling a story to demonstrate the contrast between our hearts and God's? That would certainly make sense following the parable of the prodigal son.

The shrewd manager has no redeeming qualities. He is dishonest, has no integrity, and is lazy. His master catches him stealing from him. Does he repent? No, he uses dishonest means for gain. Humans commended his shrewdness. But we are told later, "What is highly valued among men is detestable in God's sight." If we are not faithful over the little that we have, how do we expect to be given more when the Lord returns?

Jesus' teaching is clear. We cannot serve God and money. They are competing faith systems. If we love money, we will do whatever is needed to accumulate it. We do not need God in such a life, or so it seems. If we love God, we will trust him to provide, and we will have integrity in the use of that which we have at our disposal. We realize that everything we have is God's, and it has been entrusted to us.

So, what will it be? Will we prize what this world values? Will we shrewdly use what we have, thinking we can gain eternal things through dishonest gain? Surely we see the folly of such reasoning! Jesus calls us to a life of honesty, integrity, and God-honoring trust.

Since John the Baptist proclaimed the coming of the kingdom of God, people had tried to force their way into the kingdom. Jesus reminds us it comes only to those who submit to God's will. Lovers of money and material things cannot enter the kingdom, nor can those who take obedience to God's will lightly. This is why Jesus closed his discourse with a comment on divorce. Not only was money being used inappropriately and pursued as if it had eternal value, the covenant of marriage was being dismissed with alarming ease. This sounds all too familiar, does it not? Many of us need to repent from these things. If we would find true life, we must turn from this world and enter the heart of God.

"Dear Lord, free us from the love of money. May we act with integrity and honesty that brings honor to your name. May we never attempt to enter your kingdom by our own means. May we daily submit to your will."

# A WASTED LIFE

## (Luke 16:19-17:10)

### DAY ONE READING AND QUESTIONS:

[19] "There was a rich man who was dressed in purple and fine linen and lived in luxury every day. [20] At his gate was laid a beggar named Lazarus, covered with sores [21] and longing to eat what fell from the rich man's table. Even the dogs came and licked his sores.

[22] "The time came when the beggar died and the angels carried him to Abraham's side. The rich man also died and was buried. [23] In hell, where he was in torment, he looked up and saw Abraham far away, with Lazarus by his side. [24] So he called to him, 'Father Abraham, have pity on me and send Lazarus to dip the tip of his finger in water and cool my tongue, because I am in agony in this fire.'"

*1. Describe the life of the rich man. How does Lazarus' life compare?*

*2. What physically separated the two men in life?*

*3. How does the rich man address Abraham? What does this tell us about the rich man's understanding of himself?*

### DAY TWO READING AND QUESTIONS:

[25] "But Abraham replied, 'Son, remember that in your lifetime you received your good things, while Lazarus received bad things, but now

he is comforted here and you are in agony. [26] And besides all this, between us and you a great chasm has been fixed, so that those who want to go from here to you cannot, nor can anyone cross over from there to us.'

[27] "He answered, 'Then I beg you, father, send Lazarus to my father's house, [28] for I have five brothers. Let him warn them, so that they will not also come to this place of torment.'

[29] "Abraham replied, 'They have Moses and the Prophets; let them listen to them.'

[30] " 'No, father Abraham,' he said, 'but if someone from the dead goes to them, they will repent.'

[31] "He said to him, 'If they do not listen to Moses and the Prophets, they will not be convinced even if someone rises from the dead.' "

*1. Why did Abraham call the rich man "son"?*

*2. What separated Lazarus and the rich man in death?*

*3. What does the rich man's concern for others reveal about his heart? (in other words, about whom is he concerned?)*

## DAY THREE READING AND QUESTIONS:

[1] Jesus said to his disciples: "Things that cause people to sin are bound to come, but woe to that person through whom they come. [2] It would be better for him to be thrown into the sea with a millstone tied around his neck than for him to cause one of these little ones to sin. [3] So watch yourselves.

"If your brother sins, rebuke him, and if he repents, forgive him. [4] If he sins against you seven times in a day, and seven times comes back to you and says, 'I repent,' forgive him."

1. *Who are the "little ones" in this passage? (hint: consider the previous story)*

2. *What is Jesus teaching about sin and repentance?*

3. *How many times are we to forgive?*

## DAY FOUR READING AND QUESTIONS:

[5] The apostles said to the Lord, "Increase our faith!"

[6] He replied, "If you have faith as small as a mustard seed, you can say to this mulberry tree, 'Be uprooted and planted in the sea,' and it will obey you.

[7] "Suppose one of you had a servant plowing or looking after the sheep. Would he say to the servant when he comes in from the field, 'Come along now and sit down to eat'? [8] Would he not rather say, 'Prepare my supper, get yourself ready and wait on me while I eat and drink; after that you may eat and drink'? [9] Would he thank the servant because he did what he was told to do? [10] So you also, when you have done everything you were told to do, should say, 'We are unworthy servants; we have only done our duty.'"

1. *Why do you think the apostles asked for Jesus to increase their faith?*

2. *How does Jesus describe the power of faith? What does this mean?*

3. *What do you think Jesus is saying with His comments about the slave and his work?*

## DAY FIVE READING AND QUESTIONS:

Reread the entire passage (16:19-17:10).

1. *Who would be in our "circle of concern" if we found ourselves in the circumstances of the rich man? What does this say about us?*

2. *What future event is anticipated by "they will not be convinced, even if someone rises from the dead"? Are you convinced by the resurrection of Jesus that what he taught about life and wealth is true?*

3. *How do we view our work for the Lord? Do we expect special treatment, or is it the least we can do as his faithful servants?*

## MEDITATION

The story of Lazarus and the rich man is well known. However, the first ten verses of chapter seventeen are not connected often to the parable, as they are in this reading. They continue Jesus' teaching concerning the true nature of kingdom life. The rich man chose to live in self-indulged luxury, unknowingly excluding himself from God. In so doing, he caused "one of these little ones" to stumble. The little ones of chapter seventeen are not only children, but all who suffer. We must understand that Jesus is not just calling us to specific actions (caring for the poor), but to allow the Holy Spirit to give us a new heart and new eyes. New eyes would allow us to see the needs of the poor and suffering. A new heart would call us to meet those needs.

Repeatedly in Luke we have heard the call of Jesus to turn away from a life of self-centered consumerism. He warns us that such a life will end in tragedy. In this parable we see this lesson in graphic detail.

Jesus' intent is not so much to give us a picture of the afterlife, as it is to point out the inevitable result of a selfish heart. The rich man did not even notice the plight of Lazarus while they lived. Even in torment, the rich man's request demonstrates his attitude of superiority—he wanted Lazarus to serve his needs. He further demonstrated his heart by requesting Lazarus go and warn his brothers. Surely they weren't the only ones who needed to hear the warning of a life wrongly lived! Abraham's answer is important—we who are living have the word of God—that should be enough. And, as future events would show, even one raised from the dead would not be enough to turn all hearts to God.

So, how should one act with a kingdom heart? A kingdom person will have great concern for "the little ones" of the world—anyone in need—and respond appropriately. A kingdom person will be full of forgiveness and demonstrate great faith in God. Such a person will not even consider being rewarded for doing good. He or she will realize they are doing nothing more than what they should. May we have ears to hear!

"Lord of love, give us your heart and eyes. May we never be so focused on ourselves that we fail to see the needs of others."

# THE COMING OF THE KINGDOM

### (Luke 17:11-37)

## DAY ONE READING AND QUESTIONS:

[11] Now on his way to Jerusalem, Jesus traveled along the border between Samaria and Galilee. [12] As he was going into a village, ten men who had leprosy met him. They stood at a distance [13] and called out in a loud voice, "Jesus, Master, have pity on us!"

[14] When he saw them, he said, "Go, show yourselves to the priests." And as they went, they were cleansed.

[15] One of them, when he saw he was healed, came back, praising God in a loud voice. [16] He threw himself at Jesus' feet and thanked him—and he was a Samaritan.

[17] Jesus asked, "Were not all ten cleansed? Where are the other nine? [18] Was no one found to return and give praise to God except this foreigner?" [19] Then he said to him, "Rise and go; your faith has made you well."

*1. Why did the lepers "keep their distance"?*

*2. Why did Jesus ask them to "show themselves to the priests"?*

*3. Why does Luke point out that the one who turned back to thank Jesus was a Samaritan?*

## DAY TWO READING AND QUESTIONS:

[20] Once, having been asked by the Pharisees when the kingdom of God would come, Jesus replied, "The kingdom of God does not come with your careful observation, [21] nor will people say, 'Here it is,' or 'There it is,' because the kingdom of God is within you."

1. *What do you think the Pharisees meant when they asked about the coming "kingdom of God"?*

2. *Why did Jesus respond that the coming of the kingdom was not going to be things that could be observed?*

3. *What do you think Jesus meant when he said the kingdom was already among them?*

## DAY THREE READING AND QUESTIONS:

[22] Then he said to his disciples, "The time is coming when you will long to see one of the days of the Son of Man, but you will not see it. [23] Men will tell you, 'There he is!' or 'Here he is!' Do not go running off after them. [24] For the Son of Man in his day will be like the lightning, which flashes and lights up the sky from one end to the other. [25] But first he must suffer many things and be rejected by this generation.

[26] "Just as it was in the days of Noah, so also will it be in the days of the Son of Man. [27] People were eating, drinking, marrying and being given in marriage up to the day Noah entered the ark. Then the flood came and destroyed them all.

[28] "It was the same in the days of Lot. People were eating and drinking, buying and selling, planting and building. [29] But the day Lot

left Sodom, fire and sulfur rained down from heaven and destroyed them all.

[30] "It will be just like this on the day the Son of Man is revealed.

*1. What were the days of the Son of Man of which Jesus spoke?*

*2. What must happen first? Why?*

*3. How will the day of the son of Man be like those of Noah and Lot?*

## Day Four Reading and Questions:

[31] On that day no one who is on the roof of his house, with his goods inside, should go down to get them. Likewise, no one in the field should go back for anything. [32] Remember Lot's wife! [33] Whoever tries to keep his life will lose it, and whoever loses his life will preserve it. [34] I tell you, on that night two people will be in one bed; one will be taken and the other left. [35] Two women will be grinding grain together; one will be taken and the other left.'"

[37] "Where, Lord?" they asked.

He replied, "Where there is a dead body, there the vultures will gather."

*1. What are we to remember about Lot's wife?*

*2. Who will lose their lives in those days?*

*3. What do you think Jesus meant by his reference to the gathering of vultures?*

## Day Five Reading and Questions:

Go back and read the entire passage (Luke 17:11-37).

   *1. How might we be guilty of the sin of "the nine" (cleansed lepers)?*

   *2. How is the kingdom of God among us now? How does this affect our lives?*

   *3. What should be our concern about the coming of the Son of Man?*

# MEDITATION

Can you imagine what it would have been like to be a leper in Jesus' day? Considered a complete outcast, you would be slowly dying of a degenerative disease with no hope of cure. You would be forced to live in a colony, and if you wandered out, you had to shout "unclean, unclean" if anyone approached. Now imagine hearing that Jesus, the miracle worker, was passing by! Wouldn't it be easy to shout, "Master, have mercy on me"? See his smile, watch him nod his head, hear him say, "Go—show yourself to the priests." Now watch in disbelief as your body becomes whole again. The sores heal, your missing fingers grow back before your eyes, how could this be? You have been given a new life! What would you do next?

It is incomprehensible that only one was moved to thank the Healer. However, do not miss the point. While ten were healed, only one chose to experience kingdom life. Only one acknowledged the wonderful work of God, thus demonstrating his faith. Ten received healing; only one received the blessing.

We all receive uncountable blessings on a daily basis from God.

How many of us stop to thank him and acknowledge our faith in him? We call out in times of despair, and God responds generously. But the gift is too quickly forgotten as we celebrate our good fortune and continue on our way. The kingdom of God is for us, but we choose not to fall at the feet of the gentle Healer and acknowledge our thanksgiving and constant need for our Lord. If we live that way, we are missing the blessing. God doesn't need our thanksgiving, but we desperately need his blessing.

This leads us into the next story in our reading. All those around Jesus saw what he was doing. They saw the miracles, but missed the message. The clueless Pharisees asked, "When is the kingdom of God coming?" Jesus had already responded directly to this (Luke 11:20)—if he were working by the power of God (which no one could openly deny), then the kingdom of God had come! However, the Pharisees' preconceived notions concerning the kingdom of God blinded them from seeing it! They thought the kingdom was to be all about them. So the crippled could be cured, the blind given sight, the lepers cleansed, the dead raised—and it meant nothing to them! Clearly there is a second issue here. While the kingdom of God was among them in the work of Jesus, there was yet to be a final day when the kingdom would be realized in its fullness. Jesus here is dealing with two issues. The first is the Pharisees' inability to recognize who Jesus was; the second was that final day of judgment yet to come.

Jesus' discussion of his second coming contains unpleasant images. There will be some who will not be saved. There will be no second chance. We must live in the kingdom of God in the present, and then we will have no need to fear. What will happen to us on that day? Will we immediately try to grab that which we have accumulated, or will we be filled with joy because our riches have been entrusted to him who comes?

"Glorious Lord, may we live in such a way that we have no fear of your coming. Give us hearts full of thanksgiving for the cleansing we have received in Christ Jesus."

# OUR STANDING BEFORE GOD
### (Luke 18:1-17)

## DAY ONE READING AND QUESTIONS:

[1] Then Jesus told his disciples a parable to show them that they should always pray and not give up. [2] He said: "In a certain town there was a judge who neither feared God nor cared about men. [3] And there was a widow in that town who kept coming to him with the plea, 'Grant me justice against my adversary.'

[4] "For some time he refused. But finally he said to himself, 'Even though I don't fear God or care about men, [5] yet because this widow keeps bothering me, I will see that she gets justice, so that she won't eventually wear me out with her coming!' "

[6] And the Lord said, "Listen to what the unjust judge says. [7] And will not God bring about justice for his chosen ones, who cry out to him day and night? Will he keep putting them off? [8a] I tell you, he will see that they get justice, and quickly."

*1. Why did Jesus tell this parable?*

*2. Who does the judge represent in this parable?*

*3. What does the widow have going for her in this story?*

## Day Two Reading and Questions:

18b"However, when the Son of Man comes, will he find faith on the earth?"

*1. Reflect on Jesus' question. Why do you think he asked it?*

*2. What does faith have to do with asking God for things in prayer?*

*3. When is the moment to which Jesus is referring when he talks of the "Son of Man coming"?*

## Day Three Reading and Questions:

9 To some who were confident of their own righteousness and looked down on everybody else, Jesus told this parable: 10 "Two men went up to the temple to pray, one a Pharisee and the other a tax collector. 11 The Pharisee stood up and prayed about himself: 'God, I thank you that I am not like other men—robbers, evildoers, adulterers—or even like this tax collector. 12 I fast twice a week and give a tenth of all I get.'

13 "But the tax collector stood at a distance. He would not even look up to heaven, but beat his breast and said, 'God, have mercy on me, a sinner.'

14 "I tell you that this man, rather than the other, went home justified before God. For everyone who exalts himself will be humbled, and he who humbles himself will be exalted."

*1. To whom was Jesus directing this parable?*

*2. What was wrong with the Pharisee's attitude in prayer?*

*3. Who of the two was justified before God? Why?*

## Day Four Reading and Questions:

[15] People were also bringing babies to Jesus to have him touch them. When the disciples saw this, they rebuked them. [16] But Jesus called the children to him and said, "Let the little children come to me, and do not hinder them, for the kingdom of God belongs to such as these. [17] I tell you the truth, anyone who will not receive the kingdom of God like a little child will never enter it."

*1. Why would the disciples rebuke those who brought babies to Jesus to be blessed?*

*2. How do you think the kingdom of heaven belongs to those like infants?*

*3. How are we to receive the kingdom like a child?*

## Day Five Reading and Questions:

Reread the entire passage (18:1-17).

*1. What does the parable of the persistent widow teach us about prayer?*

*2. If Jesus returned right now, would you have the faith he would be seeking? Why or why not?*

*3. Which of the two praying men most closely represents your approach to prayer? How does prayer "justify" us before God?*

# MEDITATION

The question asked in the brief reading for Day Three is central to Luke's work: "When Jesus returns, will he find faith?" Will there be those with authentic faith crying out to God in those days? Do we pray full of the faith Jesus seeks?

Jesus precedes this important question with a story intended as an absurd comparison. Its purpose is to engender hope in prayer. God is nothing like the judge, and we are nothing like the widow. So, if such a hopeless person can get what she wants from an absolute scoundrel, how much more confident should we be in prayer? We are God's beloved children. He is a wonderfully generous and caring father. We can be confident that he will give us exactly what we need.

Attitude in prayer is important. Why do we go to God in prayer? Are we seeking God's help (like the publican), or are we reminding God how wonderfully faithful we are (like the Pharisee)? Only those who humble themselves before God will receive his blessings. Maybe we would never be as bold or arrogant as this Pharisee was; but is it possible that we consider ourselves better than others, and that gives us preferred standing before God? It is easy to slip into prideful prayer. Consider keeping a prayer journal, and note the content of your prayers. It is helpful to see in writing the petitions we bring before God.

How do we properly embrace the kingdom of God? We have much to learn from children in this. Watch a child receive a gift. There is no hesitation, no consideration of merit, just the joy of receiving and opening the gift! As adults, we struggle—saying things like, "Oh, no, you shouldn't have" or we begin to think about what we must do in return. Merit and status cloud our ability to celebrate. With great joy in our hearts, we need to receive the kingdom as a child. The kingdom is a free gift from God! We need to get over ourselves and celebrate like a child the gift we have been given. There is no other door.

"Joyous Giver, teach us to be as children in the receiving of your kingdom! Rid us of pride or accomplishment, that we may experience the gift of life under your reign."

# AN INVITATION TO LIFE REFUSED

## (Luke 18:18-43)

### DAY ONE READING AND QUESTIONS:

[18] A certain ruler asked him, "Good teacher, what must I do to inherit eternal life?"

[19] "Why do you call me good?" Jesus answered. "No one is good—except God alone. [20] You know the commandments: 'Do not commit adultery, do not murder, do not steal, do not give false testimony, honor your father and mother.'"

[21] "All these I have kept since I was a boy," he said.

[22] When Jesus heard this, he said to him, "You still lack one thing. Sell everything you have and give to the poor, and you will have treasure in heaven. Then come, follow me."

[23] When he heard this, he became very sad, because he was a man of great wealth. [24] Jesus looked at him and said, "How hard it is for the rich to enter the kingdom of God! [25] Indeed, it is easier for a camel to go through the eye of a needle than for a rich man to enter the kingdom of God."

1. *Why do you think the ruler addressed Jesus as "Good Teacher?" Why did Jesus not accept the salutation?*

2. *Do you think the ruler really kept the commandments? Why or why not?*

3. *Why do you think Jesus told him to sell all he had?*

## Day Two Reading and Questions:

²⁶ Those who heard this asked, "Who then can be saved?"
²⁷ Jesus replied, "What is impossible with men is possible with God."
²⁸ Peter said to him, "We have left all we had to follow you!"
²⁹ "I tell you the truth," Jesus said to them, "no one who has left home or wife or brothers or parents or children for the sake of the kingdom of God ³⁰ will fail to receive many times as much in this age and, in the age to come, eternal life."

*1. Why were the disciples so surprised by Jesus' answer to the rich ruler?*

*2. What did Jesus say was impossible? Why?*

*3. What did Jesus promise to those who left their vocations and families to follow him?*

## Day Three Reading and Questions:

³¹ Jesus took the Twelve aside and told them, "We are going up to Jerusalem, and everything that is written by the prophets about the Son of Man will be fulfilled. ³² He will be handed over to the Gentiles. They will mock him, insult him, spit on him, flog him and kill him. ³³ On the third day he will rise again."
³⁴ The disciples did not understand any of this. Its meaning was hidden from them, and they did not know what he was talking about.

*1. Why did Jesus keep reminding the disciples of his imminent death?*

*2. How much did Jesus know about the kind of treatment he would receive? Why is it important to know that Jesus knew what was coming?*

*3. In what sense was the meaning hidden from the disciples?*

## DAY FOUR READING AND QUESTIONS:

[35] As Jesus approached Jericho, a blind man was sitting by the roadside begging. [36] When he heard the crowd going by, he asked what was happening. [37] They told him, "Jesus of Nazareth is passing by."

[38] He called out, "Jesus, Son of David, have mercy on me!"

[39] Those who led the way rebuked him and told him to be quiet, but he shouted all the more, "Son of David, have mercy on me!"

[40] Jesus stopped and ordered the man to be brought to him. When he came near, Jesus asked him, [41] "What do you want me to do for you?"

"Lord, I want to see," he replied.

[42] Jesus said to him, "Receive your sight; your faith has healed you." [43] Immediately he received his sight and followed Jesus, praising God. When all the people saw it, they also praised God.

*1. What title did the blind man use that indicated he had amazing spiritual insight?*

*2. Why do you think some tried to get the man to be quiet?*

*3. Why do you think Luke included this story immediately follow the prediction of Jesus' death?*

## Day Five Reading and Questions:

Go back and read the entire passage.

1. *What do you think Jesus would ask you to give up in order to follow him and find life?*

2. *Why do you think the disciples had such a difficult time understanding Jesus' prediction of his death? Do you think there are teachings of Jesus we have yet to understand?*

3. *Why was the blind man so brash in pleading with Jesus? What can we learn from him?*

## MEDITATION

The story of those who understand the kingdom message and those who do not continues. The "eternal life" sought by the rich ruler was not life after death, but the promised life that was to accompany obedience to God in the messianic kingdom. The ruler wanted a "soft" answer, indicated by calling Jesus "good." But Jesus would have none of the word play. He reminds us that God alone is good. The ruler knew the law and claimed to have kept it since childhood. Jesus pointed out one major thing was lacking in his life—he was worshiping the wrong god! The man could not find the "good life" he wanted because he was pursuing the false god of possessions. Jesus knew just what he needed to do—get rid of that which he did not need, give it to those who needed it—and then follow Jesus. Once rid of his false god, Jesus could teach him how to live. But the rich ruler refused the invitation to life. The cost was too high.

What do each of us need to give up in order to follow Jesus? We cannot find the life for which we were created until we give up the false one we currently pursue. What would our false god be? Our vocation? Money? Status? The kingdom of God is only for those who seek it above all else.

For some, this is impossible! But with God, all is possible. The key to life is walking with Jesus. Some of us need God's miraculous help to strip away our need for anything else.

Following Jesus is not easy. Jesus again reminds his followers that his walk is leading to a cross. They have no capacity to understand. They cannot see. But there is a blind man who can see. He hears of Jesus passing by so he shouts loudly, "Jesus, son of David, have mercy on me!" Though blind, he knew the Messiah was passing by, and no one could quiet his cries for help. Because of his "sight", he was granted sight.

"Jesus, Son of David, have mercy on me. Lord, I want to see."

# AN INVITATION TO LIFE ACCEPTED

## (Luke 19:1-27)

### DAY ONE READING AND QUESTIONS:

¹ Jesus entered Jericho and was passing through. ² A man was there by the name of Zacchaeus; he was a chief tax collector and was wealthy. ³ He wanted to see who Jesus was, but being a short man he could not, because of the crowd. ⁴ So he ran ahead and climbed a sycamore-fig tree to see him, since Jesus was coming that way.

⁵ When Jesus reached the spot, he looked up and said to him, "Zacchaeus, come down immediately. I must stay at your house today." ⁶ So he came down at once and welcomed him gladly.

*1. Describe Zacchaeus.*

*2. Why do you think Zacchaeus wanted to see Jesus so badly?*

*3. What do you think Zacchaeus thought when Jesus called him by name?*

### DAY TWO READING AND QUESTIONS:

⁷ All the people saw this and began to mutter, "He has gone to be the guest of a 'sinner.' "
⁸ But Zacchaeus stood up and said to the Lord, "Look, Lord! Here

and now I give half of my possessions to the poor, and if I have cheated anybody out of anything, I will pay back four times the amount."

⁹ Jesus said to him, "Today salvation has come to this house, because this man, too, is a son of Abraham. ¹⁰ For the Son of Man came to seek and to save what was lost."

*1. What did Jesus do that upset "all the people"?*

*2. What was Zacchaeus' response to the Lord coming to his house?*

*3. What did Jesus say in response to Zacchaeus' announcement? What does this mean?*

### DAY THREE READING AND QUESTIONS:

¹¹ While they were listening to this, he went on to tell them a parable, because he was near Jerusalem and the people thought that the kingdom of God was going to appear at once. ¹² He said: "A man of noble birth went to a distant country to have himself appointed king and then to return. ¹³ So he called ten of his servants and gave them ten minas. 'Put this money to work,' he said, 'until I come back.'

¹⁴ "But his subjects hated him and sent a delegation after him to say, 'We don't want this man to be our king.'

*1. What were the people thinking that spurred the telling of this parable?*

*2. Why was the nobleman leaving town?*

*3. What does God give us to "put to work" until the Son returns?*

## Day Four Reading and Questions:

15 "He was made king, however, and returned home. Then he sent for the servants to whom he had given the money, in order to find out what they had gained with it.

16 "The first one came and said, 'Sir, your mina has earned ten more.'

17 " 'Well done, my good servant!' his master replied. 'Because you have been trustworthy in a very small matter, take charge of ten cities.'

18 "The second came and said, 'Sir, your mina has earned five more.'

19 "His master answered, 'You take charge of five cities.'

20 "Then another servant came and said, 'Sir, here is your mina; I have kept it laid away in a piece of cloth. 21 I was afraid of you, because you are a hard man. You take out what you did not put in and reap what you did not sow.'

22 "His master replied, 'I will judge you by your own words, you wicked servant! You knew, did you, that I am a hard man, taking out what I did not put in, and reaping what I did not sow? 23 Why then didn't you put my money on deposit, so that when I came back, I could have collected it with interest?'

24 "Then he said to those standing by, 'Take his mina away from him and give it to the one who has ten minas.'

25 " 'Sir,' they said, 'he already has ten!'

26 "He replied, 'I tell you that to everyone who has, more will be given, but as for the one who has nothing, even what he has will be taken away. 27 But those enemies of mine who did not want me to be king over them—bring them here and kill them in front of me.' "

*1. What happened to those who put their master's money to work?*

*2. What did the fearful servant think of his master?*

*3. What did this fear cause him to do? What was the result?*

### Day Five Reading and Questions:

Reread the entire passage (19:1-27).

*1. If Jesus called you by name and invited himself to your house, how would you respond?*

*2. What would you have to do (if anything) to have salvation pronounced on your house?*

*3. What does the parable of the minas call you to do?*

# MEDITATION

The ruler turned Jesus down. Zacchaeus, of all people, accepted the invitation to life. Luke mentions Zacchaeus by name likely because his story was well known in those days. Can you imagine—a chief tax collector—leaving everything to become a disciple of Jesus? Here is another wealthy man who had given his life to the pursuit of riches. However, unlike the rich ruler, he knew how desperately he needed to repent. Luke gives us very little information about what led Zacchaeus to give up his wealth. All we know is that Jesus called him down from the tree so they could eat at the tax collector's house. While all the people muttered at the scandal of Jesus befriending such a man, Zacchaeus cleared his soul with a shocking announcement. He would give half his possessions to the poor and repay four times the amount he had cheated people. It does not take an accountant to figure out that leaves Zacchaeus with nothing. But that did not concern

Zacchaeus in the least. He knew an offer to life when he saw it, and was not about to pass it up. In one of the last moments of joy before his death, Jesus proclaimed salvation had come to that house. Jesus could rejoice and affirm the reason for his coming—"to seek and save the lost."

The crowds around Jesus were expecting him to initiate the kingdom of God immediately. Jesus responded to those expectations with a parable. The kingdom, in its fullness, was not an imminent reality (as the Jews expected). It was like a nobleman who went on a long journey in order to be crowned king. He entrusted his possessions to his servants. There was a group of citizens who did not want him to be king. No one knew when he would return, but when he did, he would be king, and he would call for an accounting of his possessions. Those who had used his possessions for his purposes would be rewarded, those who did not would be punished. Those who were against him being king would be destroyed.

Once again Jesus warns us about the proper use of life. Make no mistake, he will return. And when he does, he will call us to account. What will we have done with what we have been given?

"Our Lord and King, may I look with joy to the time of your return. May I use what you have given me to your glory."

# TRIUMPH AND TRAGEDY

### (Luke 19:28-47)

## DAY ONE READING AND QUESTIONS:

28 After Jesus had said this, he went on ahead, going up to Jerusalem. 29 As he approached Bethphage and Bethany at the hill called the Mount of Olives, he sent two of his disciples, saying to them, 30 "Go to the village ahead of you, and as you enter it, you will find a colt tied there, which no one has ever ridden. Untie it and bring it here. 31 If anyone asks you, 'Why are you untying it?' tell him, 'The Lord needs it.' "

32 Those who were sent ahead went and found it just as he had told them. 33 As they were untying the colt, its owners asked them, "Why are you untying the colt?"

34 They replied, "The Lord needs it."

*1. Why do you think Luke provides so much detail in this scene? Why does it matter?*

*2. Do you think there is any significance in the fact that the colt had not been ridden?*

*3. What does Jesus demonstrate by telling his disciples exactly what to do and say, and the fact that it was just as he said it would be?*

## Day Two Reading and Questions:

³⁵ They brought it to Jesus, threw their cloaks on the colt and put Jesus on it. ³⁶ As he went along, people spread their cloaks on the road.

³⁷ When he came near the place where the road goes down the Mount of Olives, the whole crowd of disciples began joyfully to praise God in loud voices for all the miracles they had seen:

³⁸ "Blessed is the king who comes in the name of the Lord!"

"Peace in heaven and glory in the highest!"

³⁹ Some of the Pharisees in the crowd said to Jesus, "Teacher, rebuke your disciples!"

⁴⁰ "I tell you," he replied, "if they keep quiet, the stones will cry out."

*1. Why do you think the people responded as they did to Jesus?*

*2. What was the meaning of the acclamation given by the disciples and the crowd?*

*3. Why was Jesus told to rebuke his disciples? What was the meaning of his response to the Pharisees?*

## Day Three Reading and Questions:

⁴¹ As he approached Jerusalem and saw the city, he wept over it ⁴² and said, "If you, even you, had only known on this day what would bring you peace—but now it is hidden from your eyes. ⁴³ The days will come upon you when your enemies will build an embankment against you and encircle you and hem you in on every side. ⁴⁴ They will dash you to the ground, you and the children within your walls. They will not leave one stone on another, because you did not recognize the time of God's coming to you."

*1. Why was Jesus weeping over Jerusalem?*

*2. Why would Jerusalem receive such a severe judgment?*

*3. To what should these verses call our attention?*

## DAY FOUR READING AND QUESTIONS:

[45] Then he entered the temple area and began driving out those who were selling. [46] "It is written," he said to them, " 'My house will be a house of prayer' ; but you have made it 'a den of robbers.'"

[47] Every day he was teaching at the temple. But the chief priests, the teachers of the law and the leaders among the people were trying to kill him. [48] Yet they could not find any way to do it, because all the people hung on his words.

*1. Why do you think Jesus drove out those marketing in the temple?*

*2. Is Jesus' anger justified? Why didn't He just ask them to leave?*

*3. What did Jesus say they had done to God's house of prayer?*

## DAY FIVE READING AND QUESTIONS:

Reread the entire passage (19:28-47).

*1. How would Jesus be accepted in our cities today? How would he be accepted in our churches?*

*2. What would Jesus cry about as he looked over our cities today?*

*3. Are there ways that we have marketed religion in today's church that would offend Jesus?*

# MEDITATION

Jerusalem is on the horizon. The band of disciples and spiritual pilgrims with Jesus will soon be breaking the crest of the Mount of Olives, and the holy city will come into view. Jesus is fully aware of what is about to happen. He is willingly walking to his death.

The crowd is almost delirious with joy. Messiah is coming to receive his glory, just as the prophets had said. They cried out, "Blessed is he who comes in the name of the Lord!" This wording from Psalm 118:6 was to be reserved for Messiah, and it is for this reason that the Pharisees were furious! They wanted Jesus to rebuke those calling him "Messiah." He would not. Looking over the city, Jesus weeps. He knows what will happen to it in just a few years. The city that Jews from all over the world traveled for months to see would be reduced to unsightly rubble. It makes me wonder what Jesus would say if he were looking over our cities?

As would be expected, the triumphant procession ends at the temple. What should have been a "house of prayer" had become a "den of robbers." So Jesus drives the merchants out of the temple grounds. There was a strong tradition among the Jews that when the Messiah came, there would be a renewed focus on the purity of the temple. But in his behavior Jesus was directly threatening the system of worship that had been in place for a long time. If these merchants should not have been there, then the religious authorities should have taken care of this. Jesus "usurped" their authority with his behavior. Of course, he had every right to do so. But this was the last straw. The leaders began to plot seriously to kill him.

What do these events mean to us? They serve to bring us to the heart of the question of authentic discipleship. How will we receive Jesus? What kind of Messiah will we allow him to be? The city of Jerusalem, of all places, should have been ready to receive the Son of God. Instead, they would crucify him. As long as the people could regard him as their champion, their miracle worker, their great teacher, and as long as they could hope for personal empowerment, betterment, and a great name, they hung on his every word. In tragic irony, many who shouted, "Blessed is the king" would soon shout "Crucify him!" How could this be?

Change is uncomfortable, but essential. We will either plot against Jesus in order to keep our lives as they are, or we will fall to his feet in submission. Nothing can stay the same when Jesus enters our lives.

"Blessed is the king who comes in the name of the Lord! Peace in heaven and glory in the highest."

# THE AUTHORITY OF JESUS

(Luke 20:1-21:4)

### DAY ONE READING AND QUESTIONS:

¹ One day as he was teaching the people in the temple courts and preaching the gospel, the chief priests and the teachers of the law, together with the elders, came up to him. ² "Tell us by what authority you are doing these things," they said. "Who gave you this authority?"

³ He replied, "I will also ask you a question. Tell me, ⁴ John's baptism—was it from heaven, or from men?"

⁵ They discussed it among themselves and said, "If we say, 'From heaven,' he will ask, 'Why didn't you believe him?' ⁶ But if we say, 'From men,' all the people will stone us, because they are persuaded that John was a prophet."

⁷ So they answered, "We don't know where it was from."

⁸ Jesus said, "Neither will I tell you by what authority I am doing these things."

⁹ He went on to tell the people this parable: "A man planted a vineyard, rented it to some farmers and went away for a long time. ¹⁰ At harvest time he sent a servant to the tenants so they would give him some of the fruit of the vineyard. But the tenants beat him and sent him away empty-handed. ¹¹ He sent another servant, but that one also they beat and treated shamefully and sent away empty-handed. ¹² He sent still a third, and they wounded him and threw him out.

¹³ "Then the owner of the vineyard said, 'What shall I do? I will

send my son, whom I love; perhaps they will respect him.'

[14] "But when the tenants saw him, they talked the matter over. 'This is the heir,' they said. 'Let's kill him, and the inheritance will be ours.' [15] So they threw him out of the vineyard and killed him.

"What then will the owner of the vineyard do to them? [16] He will come and kill those tenants and give the vineyard to others."

When the people heard this, they said, "May this never be!"

17 Jesus looked directly at them and asked, "Then what is the meaning of that which is written:

" 'The stone the builders rejected

has become the capstone" ? [18] Everyone who falls on that stone will be broken to pieces, but he on whom it falls will be crushed."

[19] The teachers of the law and the chief priests looked for a way to arrest him immediately, because they knew he had spoken this parable against them. But they were afraid of the people.

1. Why did the religious leaders question Jesus' authority?

2. Why do you think Jesus refused to answer their question?

3. What was the point of the parable of the tenants? What lesson should we learn from this?

## Day Two Reading and Questions:

[20] Keeping a close watch on him, they sent spies, who pretended to be honest. They hoped to catch Jesus in something he said so that they might hand him over to the power and authority of the governor. [21] So the spies questioned him: "Teacher, we know that you speak and teach what is right, and that you do not show partiality but teach the

way of God in accordance with the truth. [22] Is it right for us to pay taxes to Caesar or not?"

[23] He saw through their duplicity and said to them, [24] "Show me a denarius. Whose portrait and inscription are on it?"

[25] "Caesar's," they replied.

He said to them, "Then give to Caesar what is Caesar's, and to God what is God's."

[26] They were unable to trap him in what he had said there in public. And astonished by his answer, they became silent.

*1. Why was Jesus asked about paying taxes?*

*2. What was Jesus' response?*

*3. The "Caesar" comment is one of the more famous sayings of Jesus. What would Jesus say today that would capture the same meaning?*

## DAY THREE READING AND QUESTIONS:

[27] Some of the Sadducees, who say there is no resurrection, came to Jesus with a question. [28] "Teacher," they said, "Moses wrote for us that if a man's brother dies and leaves a wife but no children, the man must marry the widow and have children for his brother. [29] Now there were seven brothers. The first one married a woman and died childless. [30] The second [31] and then the third married her, and in the same way the seven died, leaving no children. [32] Finally, the woman died too. [33] Now then, at the resurrection whose wife will she be, since the seven were married to her?"

[34] Jesus replied, "The people of this age marry and are given in marriage. [35] But those who are considered worthy of taking part in that age and in the resurrection from the dead will neither marry nor

be given in marriage, ³⁶ and they can no longer die; for they are like the angels. They are God's children, since they are children of the resurrection. ³⁷ But in the account of the bush, even Moses showed that the dead rise, for he calls the Lord 'the God of Abraham, and the God of Isaac, and the God of Jacob.' ³⁸ He is not the God of the dead, but of the living, for to him all are alive."

³⁹ Some of the teachers of the law responded, "Well said, teacher!" ⁴⁰ And no one dared to ask him any more questions.

1. *Why did the Sadducees ask Jesus about post-resurrection relationships if they did not believe in the resurrection?*

2. *Why did Jesus respond with his treatment of Abraham, Isaac, and Jacob?*

3. *Why did the people stop asking Jesus questions?*

### DAY FOUR READING AND QUESTIONS:

⁴¹ Then Jesus said to them, "How is it that they say the Christ is the Son of David? ⁴² David himself declares in the Book of Psalms:
" 'The Lord said to my Lord:
"Sit at my right hand
⁴³ until I make your enemies
a footstool for your feet." '
⁴⁴ David calls him 'Lord.' How then can he be his son?"

⁴⁵ While all the people were listening, Jesus said to his disciples, ⁴⁶ "Beware of the teachers of the law. They like to walk around in flowing robes and love to be greeted in the marketplaces and have the most important seats in the synagogues and the places of honor at banquets. ⁴⁷ They devour widows' houses and for a show make lengthy

prayers. Such men will be punished most severely."

[1] As he looked up, Jesus saw the rich putting their gifts into the temple treasury. [2] He also saw a poor widow put in two very small copper coins. [3] "I tell you the truth," he said, "this poor widow has put in more than all the others. [4] All these people gave their gifts out of their wealth; but she out of her poverty put in all she had to live on."

> 1. *Why do you think Jesus initiated the discussion concerning Psalm 110:1 (Luke 20:42-42)?*

> 2. *Why were the disciples to beware of the teachers of the law?*

> 3. *Did the poor widow actually put in more than the others, or was this just a figure of speech?*

## Day Five Reading and Questions:

Reread the entire passage (20:1-21:4).

> 1. *Do these teachings of Jesus threaten our present day idea of "owner-ship"? If so, in what way?*

> 2. *What is appropriate to give to our government and what should we give to God?*

> 3. *How can we give in the same way in which the widow gave? Is this possible?*

# MEDITATION

There is much to learn from Jesus on how to respond to those attempting to discredit us. First, he was asked for his source of authority. This seems absurd, unless you are asking it from the religious leaders' point of view. One simply did not state truth in those days unless it was based on a past interpretation of law. Jesus repeatedly demonstrated he was working under the direct authority of God. The questioners really did not want an answer; they were simply out to discredit him. So Jesus turned the tables and, by his reference to John, demonstrated their hypocrisy. He then answered with a parable. This one cuts to the heart of the religious leaders. There was little mystery in the interpretation of this story. The leaders were clearly the unfaithful tenants. They had to be nervous when the crowd responded to the story of the murdered son in horror, "May this never be!"

The leaders' next ploy was to trap Jesus with saying something against the Roman civil authority. If they could force this, they could have him arrested for insurrection. So he was asked about paying taxes. There was no issue with more emotional baggage in that day. Jesus calmly responded to give Caesar what Caesar was due, but to give to God what is God's. What a wonderful response! What an amazing challenge. What doesn't belong to God?

Now the Sadducees have prepared their best attack. They had the perfect question that would surely confound Jesus. What would happen to one legally married multiple times in this life, when he is resurrected in the next? Who would be his wife? For the Sadducees, this presented no problem, because they did not believe in the resurrection. Jesus quickly discredited even this question by explaining how foolish their view was, and how marriage would not be an issue in the next life. Now, even the teachers of the law were taken in. Jesus gave them an answer to use against those arrogant Sadducees. They shouted out, "Well said, teacher!"

This exchange shut the mouths of all of Jesus' critics. They knew they were outmatched. But Jesus wasn't finished. He took that which they loved most—their supposed knowledge of Scripture, and demonstrated how little they knew. His question about David and the Messiah demonstrated their view of the Anointed One was too limited. They who questioned Jesus' authority had their credibility destroyed.

He goes on to point out the shallowness of these leaders—they sought glory for themselves and even robbed widows through their desire for self-glory. We need to consider the story of the widow's gift at the treasury in this context. Her great sacrifice deeply affected Jesus. However, he also brings to light the injustice of a religious system that applauds the rich for giving much, but does not even notice the widow giving up her bread money for the day.

It is easy to condemn the religious leaders for their hardened hearts and mistaken ideas. But could this be us? Asked to faithfully give God what is rightfully his, do we jealously guard what we have? If we take all of God's blessings and use them for our own well-being, are we any different? Do we create questions that leave us justified in our own self-focused world? Do we use others to build our own personal kingdoms?

"Almighty God, Creator of all things and all people, may we live in such a way that all who know us recognize your loving and generous heart through us. Remind us that all that we have is yours."

# THE END IS COMING!

## (Luke 21:5-38)

### DAY ONE READING AND QUESTIONS:

[5] Some of his disciples were remarking about how the temple was adorned with beautiful stones and with gifts dedicated to God. But Jesus said, [6] "As for what you see here, the time will come when not one stone will be left on another; every one of them will be thrown down."

[7] "Teacher," they asked, "when will these things happen? And what will be the sign that they are about to take place?"

[8] He replied: "Watch out that you are not deceived. For many will come in my name, claiming, 'I am he,' and, 'The time is near.' Do not follow them. [9] When you hear of wars and revolutions, do not be frightened. These things must happen first, but the end will not come right away."

[10] Then he said to them: "Nation will rise against nation, and kingdom against kingdom. [11] There will be great earthquakes, famines and pestilences in various places, and fearful events and great signs from heaven.

[12] "But before all this, they will lay hands on you and persecute you. They will deliver you to synagogues and prisons, and you will be brought before kings and governors, and all on account of my name. [13] This will result in your being witnesses to them. [14] But make up your mind not to worry beforehand how you will defend yourselves. [15] For I will give you words and wisdom that none of your adversaries will be

able to resist or contradict. [16] You will be betrayed even by parents, brothers, relatives and friends, and they will put some of you to death. [17] All men will hate you because of me. [18] But not a hair of your head will perish. [19] By standing firm you will gain life.

1. *What spurred Jesus' comment about the destruction of the temple?*

2. *What things were to happen that did not signify the coming of the end?*

3. *What end was prophesied by Jesus for some of his followers? What is the difference between "death" and "perish"? (They would die but not perish).*

## Day Two Reading and Questions:

[20] "When you see Jerusalem being surrounded by armies, you will know that its desolation is near. [21] Then let those who are in Judea flee to the mountains, let those in the city get out, and let those in the country not enter the city. [22] For this is the time of punishment in fulfillment of all that has been written. [23] How dreadful it will be in those days for pregnant women and nursing mothers! There will be great distress in the land and wrath against this people. [24] They will fall by the sword and will be taken as prisoners to all the nations. Jerusalem will be trampled on by the Gentiles until the times of the Gentiles are fulfilled.

1. *How would people know when the destruction of Jerusalem was about to occur?*

2. *What were they to do when this happened?*

3. *What would happen to the city?*

## Day Three Reading and Questions:

[25] "There will be signs in the sun, moon and stars. On the earth, nations will be in anguish and perplexity at the roaring and tossing of the sea. [26] Men will faint from terror, apprehensive of what is coming on the world, for the heavenly bodies will be shaken. [27] At that time they will see the Son of Man coming in a cloud with power and great glory. [28] When these things begin to take place, stand up and lift up your heads, because your redemption is drawing near."

[29] He told them this parable: "Look at the fig tree and all the trees. [30] When they sprout leaves, you can see for yourselves and know that summer is near. [31] Even so, when you see these things happening, you know that the kingdom of God is near.

[32] "I tell you the truth, this generation will certainly not pass away until all these things have happened. [33] Heaven and earth will pass away, but my words will never pass away.

*1. What will happen as the Son of Man appears?*

*2. What did Jesus mean in his reference to a fig tree?*

*3. When would all this happen, according to Jesus?*

## Day Four Reading and Questions:

[34] "Be careful, or your hearts will be weighed down with dissipation, drunkenness and the anxieties of life, and that day will close on you unexpectedly like a trap. [35] For it will come upon all those who live on the face of the whole earth. [36] Be always on the watch, and pray that you may be able to escape all that is about to happen, and that you may be able to stand before the Son of Man."

[37] Each day Jesus was teaching at the temple, and each evening he went out to spend the night on the hill called the Mount of Olives, [38] and all the people came early in the morning to hear him at the temple.

1. *What is the point of all of Jesus' teachings in this section?*

2. *What actions does Jesus call for in anticipation of the coming of the Son of Man?*

3. *How were the people responding to the teachings of Jesus? Why were the people so willing to listen to Jesus?*

## DAY FIVE READING AND QUESTIONS:

Reread the entire passage (21:5-38).

1. *How should verses 12-19 impact us?*

2. *How does the idea of Christ's return affect your life? Is it something about which you often think? Why or why not?*

3. *For what, do you think, should we pray to be able to stand before the Son of Man?*

## MEDITATION

When the beauty of the temple caught the attention of his disciples, Jesus let them know it would not last. You would expect the follow-up question, "When, teacher?" What follows is one of the most controversial texts in Luke. Did Jesus say not only Jerusalem, but the world would pass within one generation? Jesus speaks not only of the judgment against Jerusalem, which was imminent, but also the judgment of the world at a date and time not known. The question for us is, "Are we ready to stand before the Son of Man on that day?"

We have marveled at how the religious leaders manifested a complete lack of faith in God. Their focus on their own well being and power led to the destruction of the city of Jerusalem. The "beautiful temple" was like a tomb of death. For all that it could have been, it became a symbol of Israel's well-deserved judgment. Jesus tells us that one day the world will be likewise destroyed. Does that have an impact on the way we live? Do we continue to invest our lives in that which we know will not last? When will the end come? We do not know. We do know that life is fragile, and whether the Son of Man returns within the next few minutes or we die suddenly and unexpectedly, the end has come. We are called to live in continual faithfulness, not in constant fear of eternal judgment.

Many placed their faith in the temple as the ultimate sign of God's presence in their nation, thinking mistakenly that God would never desert his house. With confidence in their approach to God rather than in God himself, they continued to live self-focused lives, which led them to crucify the author of life. Might we, too, be guilty of similar sin? With confidence in our approach to God, we allow our fleshly desires to dictate the direction of our lives. While we sing and pray of our faith in God, some of us have placed our faith in the financial dealings on Wall Street. We think we have our religion taken care of, but our hearts remain unchanged and focused on this world.

This world does not deserve our trust. As surely as Jerusalem was judged, so shall this world be destroyed. Only God merits our faith and trust. When this world begins to shake and tremble as this age passes, will we be "weighed down" by its weight, or will we "stand up and raise our heads," knowing our full redemption is near?

"Sovereign Lord, we know not the day or time of your coming. But we know you are coming. May we live to your glory every day so that we have no fear of your coming, but anticipate it with great joy!"

# THE SUPPER

## (Luke 22:1-23)

### DAY ONE READING AND QUESTIONS:

[1] Now the Feast of Unleavened Bread, called the Passover, was approaching, [2] and the chief priests and the teachers of the law were looking for some way to get rid of Jesus, for they were afraid of the people. [3] Then Satan entered Judas, called Iscariot, one of the Twelve. [4] And Judas went to the chief priests and the officers of the temple guard and discussed with them how he might betray Jesus. [5] They were delighted and agreed to give him money. [6] He consented, and watched for an opportunity to hand Jesus over to them when no crowd was present

1. *What did the religious leaders want to do and why?*

2. *What motivated Judas to betray Jesus?*

3. *Why were the religious leaders delighted with Judas and what he offered?*

### DAY TWO READING AND QUESTIONS:

[7] Then came the day of Unleavened Bread on which the Passover lamb had to be sacrificed. [8] Jesus sent Peter and John, saying, "Go and make preparations for us to eat the Passover."

[9] "Where do you want us to prepare for it?" they asked.

[10] He replied, "As you enter the city, a man carrying a jar of water will meet you. Follow him to the house that he enters, [11] and say to the owner of the house, 'The Teacher asks: Where is the guest room, where I may eat the Passover with my disciples?' [12] He will show you a large upper room, all furnished. Make preparations there."

[13] They left and found things just as Jesus had told them. So they prepared the Passover.

[14] When the hour came, Jesus and his apostles reclined at the table. [15] And he said to them, "I have eagerly desired to eat this Passover with you before I suffer. [16] For I tell you, I will not eat it again until it finds fulfillment in the kingdom of God."

*1. What did Jesus ask Peter and John to do and why?*

*2. Why did Jesus provide the detail about the man carrying water?*

*3. What was Jesus' attitude toward this supper and why?*

## DAY THREE READING AND QUESTIONS

[17] After taking the cup, he gave thanks and said, "Take this and divide it among you. [18] For I tell you I will not drink again of the fruit of the vine until the kingdom of God comes."

[19] And he took bread, gave thanks and broke it, and gave it to them, saying, "This is my body given for you; do this in remembrance of me."

*1. With what did Jesus begin "the Lord's supper," the bread or the cup?*

*2. What did Jesus mean when He said He would not drink that cup again until the kingdom came?*

*3. What did the bread represent?*

## DAY FOUR READING AND QUESTIONS:

[20] In the same way, after the supper he took the cup, saying, "This cup is the new covenant in my blood, which is poured out for you. [21] But the hand of him who is going to betray me is with mine on the table. [22] The Son of Man will go as it has been decreed, but woe to that man who betrays him." [23] They began to question among themselves which of them it might be who would do this.

*1. Why do you think Jesus mentioned his betrayer at this point?*

*2. Note the question the disciples asked among themselves and the discussion that follows (next reading).*

*3. Close your eyes and try to picture yourself at that last supper. What do you think the disciples were thinking?*

## DAY FIVE READING AND QUESTIONS

Reread the entire passage (22:1-23).

*1. When you participate in the Lord's Supper, do you picture Jesus at the table with you?*

*2. What is the most significant experience you recall at the Lord's Table?*

*3. How can we make our participation in the Lord's Supper more meaningful? What do you think Jesus wants us to remember?*

# MEDITATION

At the end of our last reading, people were gathering early in the morning during Passover week to hear Jesus teaching at the temple. The leaders were secretly meeting, trying to figure out how to do away with Jesus. They feared the crowds, so they needed some way to capture him while alone. Much to their surprise, one of his own disciples came to them and offered to betray him. With delight they quickly settled on a price. How could Judas do this? Luke only tells us that Satan entered him. In some way, the evil one convinced Judas a little money was better than kingdom life. Tragically, Satan still tells that lie, and some believe it.

While Judas conspired to betray Jesus, other disciples were preparing for a special meal. We continue to gather around that table to this day. Jesus eagerly desired this moment, knowing it would be his last fellowship with his followers before his death. Jesus sets the table with these words, "I will not eat it again until it finds fulfillment in the kingdom of God." Can you imagine what the disciples must have been thinking? Do you not think they were filled with eager expectation of the coming events? The Messianic kingdom would be established in Jerusalem, and they were right in the heart of it all!

As Jesus gave them the cup, which anticipated the coming kingdom, he again pronounced its imminent arrival. He then broke bread, the traditional way of beginning a meal, but spoke of it being his body, and they were to do this in remembrance of him. After the supper, he took the cup and spoke of the new covenant in his blood. This must have seemed like a foreign language to the disciples. It would be weeks before they would understand its significance. But we know. The Table is a sacred place of fellowship with our Lord. We are invited to renew our covenant vow to be his presence in our world.

This word "remembrance" is of great importance. It does not mean to simply recall a historical moment. Like the Passover feast, it calls to mind the mighty deliverance of God. The Jews observe Passover not as a moment of remembering the past, but as a way of becoming participants in the story—which is what we are called to do as well. The difference is we are celebrating the ultimate deliverance of God. We recall what Jesus taught and did, so that we might participate in the story with him. "Remembrance" in the biblical sense is to recall for the purpose of changing the direction of our lives. It is when we remember what Jesus did—he came in the flesh and gave us a new covenant with God through his blood—that we rededicate our lives to faithfully pursuing that covenant.

What the disciples anticipated (Jesus being crowned king) did not happen. In fact, when Jesus predicted one of them would betray him, they discussed who might do such a thing for a moment, but immediately broke into an argument about who was the greatest among them. They were still expecting an earthly kingdom to be established. Instead, they would witness the unthinkable. It would happen just as Jesus said. The results of his death and resurrection were much more spectacular than what the disciples anticipated! Kingdom? Indeed. But what a price was paid!

What do we anticipate as we gather at the Lord's Table? What is it that we request? Do we still seek the life the disciples thought they were about to receive? Or have we learned that at the Table God seeks those willing to die for him?

"Precious Savior, no words can adequately express my gratitude for the invitation to your table. Lord, change my life with my remembrance of your life and teaching. Give me the courage and strength to do whatever you call me to do to your glory."

# MISSING THE POINT

## (Luke 22:24-38)

### DAY ONE READING AND QUESTIONS:

24 Also a dispute arose among them as to which of them was considered to be greatest. 25 Jesus said to them, "The kings of the Gentiles lord it over them; and those who exercise authority over them call themselves Benefactors. 26 But you are not to be like that. Instead, the greatest among you should be like the youngest, and the one who rules like the one who serves. 27 For who is greater, the one who is at the table or the one who serves? Is it not the one who is at the table? But I am among you as one who serves.

1. *Why do you think a dispute concerning greatness broke out? (What do you think started it?)*

2. *How do Gentiles exercise authority? Why?*

3. *In what sense are we not to be like that?*

### DAY TWO READING AND QUESTIONS:

28 You are those who have stood by me in my trials. 29 And I confer on you a kingdom, just as my Father conferred one on me, 30 so that you may eat and drink at my table in my kingdom and sit on thrones, judging the twelve tribes of Israel.

*1. What did Jesus say he was giving his disciples?*

*2. What privilege would this give his disciples?*

*3. Does this promise apply to us? Why or why not, and if so, how?*

## DAY THREE READING AND QUESTIONS:

[31] "Simon, Simon, Satan has asked to sift you as wheat. [32] But I have prayed for you, Simon, that your faith may not fail. And when you have turned back, strengthen your brothers."

[33] But he replied, "Lord, I am ready to go with you to prison and to death."

[34] Jesus answered, "I tell you, Peter, before the rooster crows today, you will deny three times that you know me."

*1. Why do you think Satan asked to destroy Peter?*

*2. What did Jesus pray in response?*

*3. What did Peter's answer reflect—and why did Jesus respond as he did?*

## DAY FOUR READING AND QUESTIONS:

[35] Then Jesus asked them, "When I sent you without purse, bag or sandals, did you lack anything?"

"Nothing," they answered.

³⁶ He said to them, "But now if you have a purse, take it, and also a bag; and if you don't have a sword, sell your cloak and buy one. ³⁷ It is written: 'And he was numbered with the transgressors'; and I tell you that this must be fulfilled in me. Yes, what is written about me is reaching its fulfillment."

³⁸ The disciples said, "See, Lord, here are two swords."

"That is enough," he replied.

*1. Why did Jesus remind them of their previous mission?*

*2. Why had things now changed?*

*3. The disciples' response to this indicates they expected what?*

## Day Five Reading and Questions:

Reread the entire passage (22:24-38).

*1. Do you ever struggle with your own "greatness" and how you compare to others? How do you think Jesus would call you to resolve this?*

*2. In what sense does Jesus call us to serve? How is it possible that the one who serves is the greatest?*

*3. Do you think Satan still attempts to destroy us? What can we do to protect ourselves?*

# MEDITATION

The dispute about greatness demonstrates what the disciples still thought was about to occur. Who would be second in command in the new kingdom? Jesus, one more time, called his disciples to embrace the great reversal of the kingdom of God. Greatness is no longer in lording it over, but in serving. Jesus could say this without hesitation, for he had always lived the life of a servant. Would any of the disciples claim they were greater than he was? How about you? If you continue to pursue greatness based on this world's criteria, then you are denying the truth of Jesus' teaching. True greatness is not for the select few, but to all who will submit to God. Those who are faithful to this call are invited to the kingdom feast.

But kingdom life is not without danger. There is an enemy who lurks in the shadows desiring to destroy the faithful. Peter learned this lesson all too well. Confident he would die with Jesus if necessary, he was told he would deny ever having known him—three times that very night. Peter could not even imagine the possibility of his own failure! In fact, none of the disciples knew how bleak the coming hours would be. They actually thought they could defend Jesus with two swords! This confidence may have come from their understanding of the Lord's protection. They had seen his miracles. They had experienced kingdom power. Hey, if a couple of fish and a little bread could feed a multitude, what could two swords do to an army? With the help of God, they would conquer! The only problem is that they did not know what God was doing. Had they been able to defend Jesus, they would have thwarted the plans of God.

I wonder if we have done such in our own lives? By insisting God do what we ask instead of willingly submitting to his plans, we risk working against his plans. We do not know the way we should go, though our culture tells us we do. In times of crisis, and in times of joyful peace, we need to fall to our knees asking for guidance, instead of pulling out our tiny swords of self-direction. Self-help is a poor option when God-help is available.

"Almighty God, teach me your ways. Help me seek greatness through serving. Protect me from the evil one. Never let me stand against your will for my life."

# THE GARDEN BETRAYAL AND A DENIAL

## (Luke 22:39-71)

### DAY ONE READING AND QUESTIONS:

<sup>39</sup> Jesus went out as usual to the Mount of Olives, and his disciples followed him. <sup>40</sup> On reaching the place, he said to them, "Pray that you will not fall into temptation." <sup>41</sup> He withdrew about a stone's throw beyond them, knelt down and prayed, <sup>42</sup> "Father, if you are willing, take this cup from me; yet not my will, but yours be done." <sup>43</sup> An angel from heaven appeared to him and strengthened him. <sup>44</sup> And being in anguish, he prayed more earnestly, and his sweat was like drops of blood falling to the ground.

<sup>45</sup> When he rose from prayer and went back to the disciples, he found them asleep, exhausted from sorrow. <sup>46</sup> "Why are you sleeping?" he asked them. "Get up and pray so that you will not fall into temptation."

*1. For what did Jesus ask the disciples to pray?*

*2. For what did Jesus pray? Why do you think He prayed for this?*

*3. Are you willing to pray "not my will but yours be done" to our Father?*

### DAY TWO READING AND QUESTIONS:

<sup>47</sup> While he was still speaking a crowd came up, and the man who was called Judas, one of the Twelve, was leading them. He approached

Jesus to kiss him, [48] but Jesus asked him, "Judas, are you betraying the Son of Man with a kiss?"

[49] When Jesus' followers saw what was going to happen, they said, "Lord, should we strike with our swords?" [50] And one of them struck the servant of the high priest, cutting off his right ear.

[51] But Jesus answered, "No more of this!" And he touched the man's ear and healed him.

[52] Then Jesus said to the chief priests, the officers of the temple guard, and the elders, who had come for him, "Am I leading a rebellion, that you have come with swords and clubs? [53] Every day I was with you in the temple courts, and you did not lay a hand on me. But this is your hour—when darkness reigns."

*1. What is ironic about the way in which Judas betrayed Jesus?*

*2. How does the discussion regarding the swords come back into play? What is surprising about the healing scene in the middle of this dramatic arrest?*

*3. What was Jesus' question to those who arrested him? Why did he ask this?*

## Day Three Reading and Questions:

[54] Then seizing him, they led him away and took him into the house of the high priest. Peter followed at a distance. [55] But when they had kindled a fire in the middle of the courtyard and had sat down together, Peter sat down with them. [56] A servant girl saw him seated there in the firelight. She looked closely at him and said, "This man was with him."

[57] But he denied it. "Woman, I don't know him," he said.

[58] A little later someone else saw him and said, "You also are one of them."

"Man, I am not!" Peter replied.

[59] About an hour later another asserted, "Certainly this fellow was with him, for he is a Galilean."

[60] Peter replied, "Man, I don't know what you're talking about!" Just as he was speaking, the rooster crowed. [61] The Lord turned and looked straight at Peter. Then Peter remembered the word the Lord had spoken to him: "Before the rooster crows today, you will disown me three times." [62] And he went outside and wept bitterly.

1. *Why do you think Peter followed Jesus to the high priest's house?*

2. *What is the progression of Peter's denials? What does this show?*

3. *How do you think the Lord looked at Peter—with condemnation or sorrow? Why?*

## DAY FOUR READING AND QUESTIONS:

[63] The men who were guarding Jesus began mocking and beating him. [64] They blindfolded him and demanded, "Prophesy! Who hit you?" [65] And they said many other insulting things to him.

[66] At daybreak the council of the elders of the people, both the chief priests and teachers of the law, met together, and Jesus was led before them. [67] "If you are the Christ,'" they said, "tell us."

Jesus answered, "If I tell you, you will not believe me, [68] and if I asked you, you would not answer. [69] But from now on, the Son of Man will be seated at the right hand of the mighty God."

[70] They all asked, "Are you then the Son of God?"

He replied, "You are right in saying I am."

⁷¹ Then they said, "Why do we need any more testimony? We have heard it from his own lips."

1. *Why did the council want Jesus to tell them he was the Christ? Why did he refuse to answer them?*

2. *Why did he acknowledge being the Son of God?*

3. *What can we learn from Jesus' behavior before his accusers?*

### Day Five Reading and Questions:

Reread the entire passage (22:39-71).

1. *Do you ever pray to "not fall into temptation"? If so, have you found it helpful in the battle against Satan?*

2. *How do you think Jesus looks at you? Why do you think this?*

3. *What are ways we might deny knowing Jesus in today's world? Have you ever denied knowing Jesus? Have you repented?*

## MEDITATION

Every believer needs to walk with Jesus to the garden. Here we see the full humanity of Jesus. He knew what was coming. He asked that it be taken away, if at all possible. The cup he dreaded was the anguish of separation from his father. Could salvation be accomplished in some other way? No, it would require Jesus to follow the plan. Calvary was not optional. So Jesus yielded his will to his Father's. Ultimately, each authentic disciple must say, "Not my will, but yours be done." This is the goal of all spiritual disciplines—to learn to submit fully to the will of God in every situation in life.

We have reached the climax of Jesus' example of faithfulness. His willingness to submit did not come from one night of prayer, but from a life of constant prayer. He could trust his father because of their intimate relationship formed over years of conversation. In stark contrast to Jesus, we see those he referred to as "little faiths"—his disciples. In their reality, sleep took precedence over prayer. When the moment of trial came, they were not equipped with the prayerful wisdom needed to respond appropriately. When first threatened, they were ready to fight, only to find out that was not appropriate. While the others fled, Peter followed at a distance. His failure over the next few hours would be most painful. Luke tells us Jesus looked at Peter after his third denial. That look broke Peter's heart.

Jesus' trials were only just beginning. The amount of abuse he was willing to bear is beyond our ability to understand. Isaiah 50:4-9 foretells why he could suffer such pain—Jesus knew his father was near. One cannot help but be deeply impressed by the strength and resolve of Jesus. In all that happened, he never wavered. He did not feel the need to defend himself. His father was in control of all that happened. He had committed himself to obey.

How do you respond when mocked? How do you respond when one uses coercive power over you in an inappropriate way? How do you act when called to suffer? We have so much to learn from Jesus! But if we want to learn to live like Jesus, we must be willing to train to live like Jesus. If we choose to live in the world of the disciples that night, we had better sharpen our swords. But if we instead accept Jesus' invitation to live in the world where God is in control and God is near, all we need is faith. But such faith demands intimate relationship with God, one strengthened by many hours of intentionally walking together.

"Sovereign Lord, teach me to fully submit my will to yours. Give me the wisdom to constantly seek you in all the events of my life."

# SENTENCED TO DIE

## (Luke 23:1-25)

### DAY ONE READING AND QUESTIONS:

[1] Then the whole assembly rose and led him off to Pilate. [2] And they began to accuse him, saying, "We have found this man subverting our nation. He opposes payment of taxes to Caesar and claims to be Christ, a king."

[3] So Pilate asked Jesus, "Are you the king of the Jews?"

"Yes, it is as you say," Jesus replied.

[4] Then Pilate announced to the chief priests and the crowd, "I find no basis for a charge against this man."

[5] But they insisted, "He stirs up the people all over Judea by his teaching. He started in Galilee and has come all the way here."

[6] On hearing this, Pilate asked if the man was a Galilean. [7] When he learned that Jesus was under Herod's jurisdiction, he sent him to Herod, who was also in Jerusalem at that time.

*1. Of what was Jesus accused? Why is this so ironic?*

*2. What was Pilate's initial judgment on Jesus? Why?*

*3. What let Pilate "off the hook"—at least for a while?*

## Day Two Reading and Questions:

⁸ When Herod saw Jesus, he was greatly pleased, because for a long time he had been wanting to see him. From what he had heard about him, he hoped to see him perform some miracle. ⁹ He plied him with many questions, but Jesus gave him no answer. ¹⁰ The chief priests and the teachers of the law were standing there, vehemently accusing him. ¹¹ Then Herod and his soldiers ridiculed and mocked him. Dressing him in an elegant robe, they sent him back to Pilate. ¹² That day Herod and Pilate became friends—before this they had been enemies.

*1. What pleased Herod about seeing Jesus?*

*2. What did Herod hope to see?*

*3. What was the result of Jesus' visit to Herod?*

## Day Three Reading and Questions:

¹³ Pilate called together the chief priests, the rulers and the people, ¹⁴ and said to them, "You brought me this man as one who was inciting the people to rebellion. I have examined him in your presence and have found no basis for your charges against him. ¹⁵ Neither has Herod, for he sent him back to us; as you can see, he has done nothing to deserve death. ¹⁶ Therefore, I will punish him and then release him.'"
¹⁸ With one voice they cried out, "Away with this man! Release Barabbas to us!" ¹⁹ (Barabbas had been thrown into prison for an insurrection in the city, and for murder.)

*1. What was Pilate's second judgment on Jesus and what was his reasoning for it?*

*2. What did Pilate offer to do to Jesus and why?*

*3. Why it is ironic that Barabbas was released rather than Jesus?*

## Day Four Reading and Questions:

[20] Wanting to release Jesus, Pilate appealed to them again. [21] But they kept shouting, "Crucify him! Crucify him!"

[22] For the third time he spoke to them: "Why? What crime has this man committed? I have found in him no grounds for the death penalty. Therefore I will have him punished and then release him."

[23] But with loud shouts they insistently demanded that he be crucified, and their shouts prevailed. [24] So Pilate decided to grant their demand. [25] He released the man who had been thrown into prison for insurrection and murder, the one they asked for, and surrendered Jesus to their will.

*1. Why do you think the people were so set on crucifying Jesus?*

*2. Why did Pilate ultimately give in?*

*3. How could people who, just a few days before, acknowledged Jesus as Messiah now call for his death?*

## Day Five Reading and Questions:

Reread the entire passage (23:1-25).

*1. What affects you most from the story of the arrest and trial of Jesus?*

2. *Try to place yourself in Pilate's shoes. What do you think you would have done?*

3. *Have you ever been falsely accused? If so, how did you respond?*

# MEDITATION

The leaders take Jesus to Pilate to secure permission to kill Jesus. Luke is clear in letting us know that Pilate found no fault in Jesus. He attempted to resolve his dilemma by sending Jesus to Herod. Herod's treatment of Jesus is deeply troubling for the believer. He trivialized Jesus as a sideshow of carnival magic. When Jesus refused to entertain, Herod and his soldiers then began to mock him. Jesus' self-control is amazing. He willingly accepted the scorn and the shame.

Pilate, after Herod sent Jesus back to him, attempted to reason with the Jewish leaders, citing the lack of evidence to substantiate their accusations. Pilate offered to beat Jesus, which was a significant concession. Though deemed innocent, Pilate was willing to bring him to the verge of death just to satisfy the Jews. It was the persistence of the crowd that convinced Pilate to allow them to kill Jesus. Their shouts, "Crucify him!" prevailed.

How could this happen? How could the crowd who shouted, "Blessed is he who comes in the name of the Lord! Hosanna!" now shout, "Crucify him! Crucify Him!"? Some have suggested these were two different crowds. The crowd wanting Jesus crucified was a crowd selected by the Jewish leaders in order to accomplish their purposes. But the text suggests it was the same general crowd. They were willing to acknowledge Jesus as Messiah as long as he met their expectations. The turning point was when Jesus submitted to Pilate's judgment. While Pilate was desperately trying to release Jesus, Jesus was not attempting to overthrow Pilate. Anyone with sense at all knew the

Messiah was coming to free the Jews from Roman oppression! Or at least, so thought the common Jewish pilgrim, ready to celebrate and crown the Messiah as king. One who would not even open his mouth in defense of the charges brought against him had to be a powerless fraud!

What do we do with this part of the story of Jesus' trial? There are personal lessons to learn. First, have we ever manipulated the facts to make sure we get our way in a conflict? Surely, we see the ugliness of human nature in the "trial" of Jesus. The Jewish leaders were so intent on killing him they were willing to do whatever necessary to see that it was done. We shudder at their lack of integrity. But we need to make sure we do not participate in their deed by doing similar things in lesser ways.

Second, we have to be impressed with Jesus' integrity and strength. Most evident is his unwavering faith in God. He subjected himself to every possible form of abuse, and though he had the power to strike back, he did not. Peter tells us this is the example he left for us (1 Peter 1:21)—to suffer and not seek vindication. Only in a world where God is involved would Jesus' behavior make sense. We seek to defend ourselves and defend our rights likely because we do not think God will do so. Jesus left us an example of incredible faith.

Third, we must make sure that we do not fall to the same sin that overcame the crowd. We shouldn't turn away from God simply because he does not act the way we think he should. The problem with the people's understanding of the Messiah was that their vision was too limited. They wanted a national king, and God was providing an eternal Savior. In my years of ministry I have seen many turn away from God because he did not respond as they insisted. If God would allow his Son to die so that we might have life, should we not be willing to give our all to submit to *his* will?

"Sovereign God, increase my faith to suffer without seeking vindication. May I trust you, denying the urge to manipulate others for my purposes."

# CRUCIFIED AND BURIED

## (Luke 23:26-56)

### Day One Reading and Questions:

<sup>26</sup> As they led him away, they seized Simon from Cyrene, who was on his way in from the country, and put the cross on him and made him carry it behind Jesus. <sup>27</sup> A large number of people followed him, including women who mourned and wailed for him. <sup>28</sup> Jesus turned and said to them, "Daughters of Jerusalem, do not weep for me; weep for yourselves and for your children. <sup>29</sup> For the time will come when you will say, 'Blessed are the barren women, the wombs that never bore and the breasts that never nursed!' <sup>30</sup> Then

'they will say to the mountains, "Fall on us!"

and to the hills, "Cover us!"' <sup>31</sup> For if men do these things when the tree is green, what will happen when it is dry?"

*1. What strikes you most about the scene described in these verses?*

*2. What was Jesus' concern and why?*

*3. What event was Jesus foretelling?*

### Day Two Reading and Questions:

<sup>32</sup> Two other men, both criminals, were also led out with him to be

executed. ³³ When they came to the place called the Skull, there they crucified him, along with the criminals—one on his right, the other on his left. ³⁴ Jesus said, "Father, forgive them, for they do not know what they are doing." And they divided up his clothes by casting lots.

³⁵ The people stood watching, and the rulers even sneered at him. They said, "He saved others; let him save himself if he is the Christ of God, the Chosen One."

³⁶ The soldiers also came up and mocked him. They offered him wine vinegar ³⁷ and said, "If you are the king of the Jews, save yourself."

³⁸ There was a written notice above him, which read: THIS IS THE KING OF THE JEWS.

³⁹ One of the criminals who hung there hurled insults at him: "Aren't you the Christ? Save yourself and us!"

⁴⁰ But the other criminal rebuked him. "Don't you fear God," he said, "since you are under the same sentence? ⁴¹ We are punished justly, for we are getting what our deeds deserve. But this man has done nothing wrong."

⁴² Then he said, "Jesus, remember me when you come into your kingdom.'"

⁴³ Jesus answered him, "I tell you the truth, today you will be with me in paradise."

*1. How are those around Jesus during his crucifixion described?*

*2. What was Jesus' concern in these verses?*

*3. Why is the witness of the repentant thief so precious to the believer? How do you think the dying thief knew so much about Jesus and his kingdom?*

## Day Three Reading and Questions:

[44] It was now about the sixth hour, and darkness came over the whole land until the ninth hour, [45] for the sun stopped shining. And the curtain of the temple was torn in two. [46] Jesus called out with a loud voice, "Father, into your hands I commit my spirit." When he had said this, he breathed his last.

[47] The centurion, seeing what had happened, praised God and said, "Surely this was a righteous man." [48] When all the people who had gathered to witness this sight saw what took place, they beat their breasts and went away. [49] But all those who knew him, including the women who had followed him from Galilee, stood at a distance, watching these things.

*1. What events happened as Jesus was dying? What do these things tell us?*

*2. What is significant about the last words of Jesus?*

*3. What do you think caused the centurion to praise God in the events of Jesus' death?*

## Day Four Reading and Questions:

[50] Now there was a man named Joseph, a member of the Council, a good and upright man, [51] who had not consented to their decision and action. He came from the Judean town of Arimathea and he was waiting for the kingdom of God. [52] Going to Pilate, he asked for Jesus' body. [53] Then he took it down, wrapped it in linen cloth and placed it in a tomb cut in the rock, one in which no one had yet been laid. [54] It was Preparation Day, and the Sabbath was about to begin.

55 The women who had come with Jesus from Galilee followed Joseph and saw the tomb and how his body was laid in it. 56 Then they went home and prepared spices and perfumes. But they rested on the Sabbath in obedience to the commandment.

 *1. Why do you think Luke mentioned Joseph's position in the Council?*

 *2. How do you think the followers of Jesus must have felt as his body was taken down and prepared for burial?*

 *3. Have you experienced times of deep trial in your life when you thought all was lost? How did God deliver you?*

### Day Five Reading and Questions:

Reread the entire passage (23:26-56).

 *1. If you knew you were going to die, what would you want those you love most to know?*

 *2. Picture yourself as the second thief. What would you say to Jesus?*

 *3. What event or words in the story of Jesus' death leave the deepest impact on your life? Why?*

# MEDITATION

Even in these terrible, final moments, Jesus' concern was for those around him. For once, we would think, he should be thinking about himself. Luke wants us to know that Jesus died in the same spirit in which he lived. He was a living sacrifice his entire ministry; now he is willing to die as a sacrifice. He turned to the women mourning and told them to weep not for him but for an unbelieving city. As the scene builds in unthinkable violence against the Lamb of God, his cry is for God's forgiveness for those abusing him.

Jesus is shamed beyond what we could imagine. Not only is he beaten and stripped, but is placed between two lowly criminals to die. Jeering crowds surround him, mocking his apparent weakness. Can you imagine having the power to stop all of this and choosing not to? What the world saw as powerlessness was instead the greatest demonstration of power in human history. Though he had the power to retaliate, he demonstrated true strength by not vindicating himself. In giving himself to die, he embodied his message to the world, "If you want to save your life, you must lose it." By entrusting himself fully and completely to God, he demonstrated the true power of the kingdom—self-death in exchange for life. The soldiers who mocked Jesus with the words, "If you are king of the Jews, then save yourself," did not realize their statement was a deep contradiction. It was because Jesus was king of the Jews that he would not save himself. For in giving himself, he saved all who would place their faith in him.

As Jesus took his last breath, he called out with a loud voice a phrase that summarizes his life in a powerful way, "Father, into your hands I commit my spirit." It is a moment that touches the very bottom of our hearts and moves us to tears. Throughout the faithful son's intense and extended time of suffering, he never loses his sense of sonship. The Father is still his father, and he lovingly commits all he has left to his father, who will do what is right. Could we say with Jesus, "Father, I give you my life"?

We know the rest of the story. But it is important to remember how bleak this moment in history must have been for the followers of Jesus. Their lives were shattered, their hopes destroyed, their aspirations for the kingdom buried with their Lord. Though they did not know it, a new day was about to dawn. But there would be deep agony before absolute victory. So it is in the kingdom. God does some of his greatest work when it looks like the enemy has won. For those who choose to walk with God, the outcome is inevitable. We have suffered through Friday, but Sunday is coming.

"Merciful Lord, what can we possibly say? We are moved beyond words at what Jesus endured for us. Give us the resolve to die with Jesus, and be raised by your power to kingdom life."

# RESURRECTION!

## (Luke 24:1-12)

### DAY ONE READING AND QUESTIONS:

[1] On the first day of the week, very early in the morning, the women took the spices they had prepared and went to the tomb. [2] They found the stone rolled away from the tomb, [3] but when they entered, they did not find the body of the Lord Jesus.

1. *Why did the women wait for the first day of the week to prepare Jesus' body?*

2. *What do you think the women thought when they saw the stone rolled away from the door?*

3. *Can you imagine walking into the tomb and seeing the body was not there? Try your best to put yourself in the tomb, experience the confusion and possible hope that was sparked in the hearts of the women on that Sunday morning.*

### DAY TWO READING AND QUESTIONS:

[4] While they were wondering about this, suddenly two men in clothes that gleamed like lightning stood beside them. [5] In their fright the women bowed down with their faces to the ground, but the men said to them, "Why do you look for the living among the dead?

*1. Why did the men frighten the women?*

*2. What is significant about the question the men asked the women?*

*3. Is it possible that we, too, sometimes think of Jesus as dead rather than alive?*

## DAY THREE READING AND QUESTIONS:

⁶ He is not here; he has risen! Remember how he told you, while he was still with you in Galilee: ⁷ 'The Son of Man must be delivered into the hands of sinful men, be crucified and on the third day be raised again.' " ⁸ Then they remembered his words.

*1. "He is not here; he has risen!" has been called the most important proclamation in all of history. Do you agree? Why or why not?*

*2. Why do you think the angels recalled Jesus' words predicting His death?*

*3. What emotion do you think the women experienced most strongly as they "remembered His words"?*

## DAY FOUR READING AND QUESTIONS:

⁹ When they came back from the tomb, they told all these things to the Eleven and to all the others. ¹⁰ It was Mary Magdalene, Joanna, Mary the mother of James, and the others with them who told this to the apostles. ¹¹ But they did not believe the women, because their words seemed to them like nonsense. ¹² Peter, however, got up and ran

to the tomb. Bending over, he saw the strips of linen lying by themselves, and he went away, wondering to himself what had happened.

1. *Why does Luke mention "the Eleven"?*

2. *Why did the eleven not believe the women's testimony?*

3. *How did Peter react to the news?*

### Day Five Reading and Questions:

Reread the entire passage (24:1-12).

1. *How does this reading affect you?*

2. *Why did it take so long to understand the words of Jesus about his death?*

3. *Are there words of Jesus that for a long time you were not able to hear? What caused you to understand those words?*

## MEDITATION

The importance of the resurrection cannot be overstated. For the believer in Jesus, it is everything. It is the vindication of all of Jesus' teaching and of His death itself. Many have given their life in martyrdom; only one has risen to demonstrate that the power of death has been broken. Satan has been defeated!

To this day, we meet together on "resurrection day" to celebrate this great victory. The most astounding experience of joy ever celebrated on this earth is surely when Jesus' followers came to understand what had happened. Walk with the faithful women to the tomb, experience the deep dread they must have anticipated in handling the stiff and decaying body of their Lord. Imagine how difficult it must have been to realize they would be forced to see his lifeless and scarred body. Now, look up as you approach the tomb and see with anxiety the stone rolled away. What do you expect to find? Do you pick up the pace when you see the open tomb? Now you enter and are shocked to see the body is gone! "What has happened? Has someone taken the body?"

Now hear the words of the gleaming men (surely angels!), words that would change the world, *"Why do you look for the living among the dead? He is not here; he is risen! Remember how he told you...."* YES! We remember! He told us about this! How did we not hear this? How many times did he tell us? Now you cannot help but run! The others must know! The world must know—**HE IS RISEN!**

We need to experience this moment. Stop reading! Pump your fists to the sky in joyful celebration! Satan is defeated! Death is destroyed! This is our moment of victory!

Do you think about these events often? What does the resurrection mean to you? Paul said without it, we are miserable people. But, since we know He is risen, we are full of hope and joy. Every word spoken by Jesus is true. So now, we have everything we need for life. We have the truth embodied in a Savior who gave himself as a sacrifice for my sins, and is risen to give me a confident hope of new life in him. The power that raised Jesus from the dead can also raise me up from my sins and lead me to new life.

Celebrate the resurrection. It is God's gift to humanity. We know that we will never die, because Jesus has died for us. God rolled the stone away. The grave clothes lie on the floor of the empty tomb. Do not look for Jesus there. The living Lord has no place in a dark tomb. Hallelujah!

"Lord of life, we celebrate with you the great moment of resurrection! Thank you for life! May the world know you are risen by the lives we live for you."

# THE GREATEST SERMON EVER PREACHED

## (Luke 24:13-53)

### Day One Reading and Questions:

¹³ Now that same day two of them were going to a village called Emmaus, about seven miles from Jerusalem. ¹⁴ They were talking with each other about everything that had happened. ¹⁵ As they talked and discussed these things with each other, Jesus himself came up and walked along with them; ¹⁶ but they were kept from recognizing him.

¹⁷ He asked them, "What are you discussing together as you walk along?"

They stood still, their faces downcast. ¹⁸ One of them, named Cleopas, asked him, "Are you only a visitor to Jerusalem and do not know the things that have happened there in these days?"

¹⁹ "What things?" he asked.

"About Jesus of Nazareth," they replied. "He was a prophet, powerful in word and deed before God and all the people.

*1. Why do you think Jesus chose to walk with these troubled disciples?*

*2. Why did the disciples fail to recognize Jesus?*

*3. Who was Jesus, for them, at this point?*

## Day Two Reading and Questions:

[20] The chief priests and our rulers handed him over to be sentenced to death, and they crucified him; [21] but we had hoped that he was the one who was going to redeem Israel. And what is more, it is the third day since all this took place. [22] In addition, some of our women amazed us. They went to the tomb early this morning [23] but didn't find his body. They came and told us that they had seen a vision of angels, who said he was alive. [24] Then some of our companions went to the tomb and found it just as the women had said, but him they did not see."

[25] He said to them, "How foolish you are, and how slow of heart to believe all that the prophets have spoken! [26] Did not the Christ have to suffer these things and then enter his glory?" [27] And beginning with Moses and all the Prophets, he explained to them what was said in all the Scriptures concerning himself.

[28] As they approached the village to which they were going, Jesus acted as if he were going farther. [29] But they urged him strongly, "Stay with us, for it is nearly evening; the day is almost over." So he went in to stay with them.

[30] When he was at the table with them, he took bread, gave thanks, broke it and began to give it to them. [31] Then their eyes were opened and they recognized him, and he disappeared from their sight. [32] They asked each other, "Were not our hearts burning within us while he talked with us on the road and opened the Scriptures to us?"

[33] They got up and returned at once to Jerusalem. There they found the Eleven and those with them, assembled together [34] and saying, "It is true! The Lord has risen and has appeared to Simon." [35] Then the two told what had happened on the way, and how Jesus was recognized by them when he broke the bread.

*1. What was once the hope of these disciples, and why had they lost it?*

*2. What report amazed them and why?*

*3. When did they recognize Jesus? What was their response?*

## DAY THREE READING AND QUESTIONS:

[36] While they were still talking about this, Jesus himself stood among them and said to them, "Peace be with you."
[37] They were startled and frightened, thinking they saw a ghost. [38] He said to them, "Why are you troubled, and why do doubts rise in your minds? [39] Look at my hands and my feet. It is I myself! Touch me and see; a ghost does not have flesh and bones, as you see I have."
[40] When he had said this, he showed them his hands and feet. [41] And while they still did not believe it because of joy and amazement, he asked them, "Do you have anything here to eat?" [42] They gave him a piece of broiled fish, [43] and he took it and ate it in their presence.

*1. What does "peace" have to do with Jesus and what did he mean when he conferred it on his disciples?*

*2. Why is it important that Jesus was not a "ghost" or "spirit"?*

*3. Why do you think Jesus ate food in their presence?*

## DAY FOUR READING AND QUESTIONS:

[44] He said to them, "This is what I told you while I was still with you: Everything must be fulfilled that is written about me in the Law

of Moses, the Prophets and the Psalms."

⁴⁵ Then he opened their minds so they could understand the Scriptures. ⁴⁶ He told them, "This is what is written: The Christ will suffer and rise from the dead on the third day, ⁴⁷ and repentance and forgiveness of sins will be preached in his name to all nations, beginning at Jerusalem. ⁴⁸ You are witnesses of these things. ⁴⁹ I am going to send you what my Father has promised; but stay in the city until you have been clothed with power from on high."

⁵⁰ When he had led them out to the vicinity of Bethany, he lifted up his hands and blessed them. ⁵¹ While he was blessing them, he left them and was taken up into heaven. ⁵² Then they worshiped him and returned to Jerusalem with great joy. ⁵³ And they stayed continually at the temple, praising God.

1. *What is the interpretive key to all of the scriptures according to Jesus?*

2. *How is the "great commission" given in Luke's gospel?*

3. *What was the result of Jesus' ascension in the life of his disciples?*

## Day Five Reading and Questions:

Reread the entire passage (24:13-53).

1. *Have you ever been so disappointed that you failed to see the work of God in a particular event? Reflect on what you learned from that experience.*

2. *How often do you think of the risen, exalted Jesus Christ as you live your life of praise to him?*

3. *What is the most significant truth you have learned in this journey through Luke?*

# MEDITATION

The Lord is risen! If you were writing the story, where would Jesus go? I would have him first appear in the middle of the Sanhedrin. I would have Jesus dare them to mock him now! Or how about Jesus appearing in the temple courts, asking people what they now thought of him? I would at least have him dealing out a little punishment on the Roman soldiers who crucified him. But the resurrected Lord continues to live consistently with his nature before his death. He is not interested in the spectacular. He would rather walk with two struggling disciples who were trying to make sense of it all. That means he will walk with me and with you when it's hard to make sense of life.

I am so thankful to Luke for this marvelous story. It should greatly encourage all of us. Jesus walks with those struggling to make sense of their faith; he does not abandon them. Their hearts were broken, their minds confused, their hopes dashed. Can you hear their words to one another before the "stranger" joined them? A remembered teaching, a retelling of a wonderful miracle, then silence—how could he have been crucified? Then Jesus (his identity hidden from them) asked them to explain to him why they were troubled. After hearing their retelling of the events, Jesus shared with them what has to be the greatest sermon ever heard.

For the first time, Jesus, the eternal word of God, told the entire story. God's dramatic narrative of redemption was now fully revealed! The disciples' minds were opened, and it caused their hearts to burn. Does the story burn in our hearts? Can we start from the beginning and see how everything points us to the Christ? Do we see this story as our story?

You have to love the way Jesus finally reveals himself to his companions on the road. Arriving at Emmaus, they invited him to their house where he strangely assumed the role of host. He took the bread, gave thanks, and broke it with them. Then they knew! What a moment that must have been! Sit at their table. Watch his hands break the bread. Feel the thrill of new hope, of broken hearts healed, of new life! Do not lose that sense of true excitement!

As Jesus revealed himself to those who followed him, he commissioned them to continue his work. This is the story that Luke continues in Acts. One more time Jesus tells them the true story of redemption, which finally, finally, they can understand. "This is what is written: The Christ will suffer...." How well do we know the story? How does this story of Jesus impact you? I would highly recommend that you take the time to reread Luke—and do it in one setting. Reflect on what you have learned from Jesus, and you will surely learn to love him more. It is a marvelous story. It is our story. Jesus is risen! Hallelujah! It is our joy and privilege to tell the story of life. Jesus is savior, indeed!

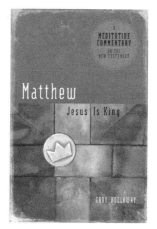
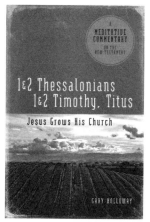
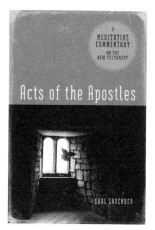
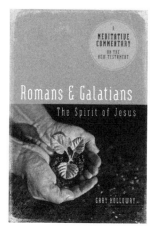